REVISED EDITION
Great Quarterbacks #1

Staubach·Landry
Plunkett·Gabriel

by Bill Gutman

tempo
books

GROSSET & DUNLAP
Publishers   New York

ISBN: 0-448-07428-1
Tempo Books is registered in the U.S. Patent Office

A Tempo Books Original

Printed in the United States of America

To my Mother and Father

ACKNOWLEDGMENTS

The author wishes to thank the following people for their help in supplying background material for this book:

Joe Browne and Kay O'Reilly, of the National Football League office; Curt Mosher of the Dallas Cowboys; the publicity departments of all four NFL teams represented; Frank Weedon and Budd Thalman, sports information directors at North Carolina State and the Naval Academy respectively; the sports information department at the University of Massachusetts; college coaches Wayne Hardin and Earl Edwards; Robert Woolf and Edward Masry; and the quarterbacks who talked freely about their experiences as star football players.

Contents

Jim Plunkett

It was the last game of the New England Patriots' 1971 season, and the final game of Jim Plunkett's rookie year. The team was up against the division-leading Baltimore Colts, at Baltimore's Memorial Stadium. With a little more than two minutes left in the game, the score was a surprising 14-10 in favor of the Pats. Would they be able to upset the favored Colts?

The Patriots were huddled close to their own goal line, the ball resting out at the 12. It was a third-down play, with a big twelve yards to go. If the Pats got a first down, they might be able to run out the clock and turn their lead into a victory. If the Colts could force New England to punt, Baltimore would get the ball at about midfield. That's what the Colt fans wanted. They knew that their 38-year-old quarterback, the great John Unitas, was still a master at marching his team downfield in no time flat.

The tough Baltimore defense waited. It was a veteran unit, one that almost always held on a key play. Now they were digging in, ready to get that ball for Unitas if they had to run over every Patriot to do it.

In the huddle, Jim Plunkett had to make a decision.

1

It wasn't an easy one for a rookie quarterback. He knew about Unitas, too. But picking up 12 yards this deep in Colt territory was no easy task. He could play it safe and try a draw or sweep, which surely wouldn't get him the first down. Then he could punt and hope his defense held. Or he could gamble.

Jim Plunkett wasn't one to turn away from a challenge. He decided to gamble. Looking across the huddle at his favorite wide receiver, Randy Vataha, Plunkett said just one word . . .

. . . "Go!"

The rest of the Pats knew what that meant. Plunkett would try to throw the Colt defense off balance by faking a run, then he'd go deep to Vataha. A gamble, yes. But at this stage of the game, a good one.

Center Jon Morris got down over the ball, and Plunkett barked the signals in a crisp, confident voice. At the snap, the two lines thudded together and Plunkett faked a handoff to his fullback, Jim Nance. He hid the ball on his hip as he dropped back, set himself for a split second, then whipped his powerful right arm forward, hurling the football as far as he could.

All eyes at Baltimore's Memorial Stadium looked downfield. There was Vataha, sprinting five yards in front of Colt defenders Rex Kern and Rick Volk. The only question now was would he catch up with the football?

Vataha looked over his left shoulder and saw the ball coming down. He ran just a little harder and felt it settle into his sure hands. Without breaking stride, he caught the ball and sprinted to the goal line, far ahead of his desperate pursuers.

Touchdown, Patriots!

The extra point was the icing on the cake. The Pats were 21-10 winners, knocking the Colts out of first place, and finishing their own season with a 6-8 record, a dramatic improvement over the previous year's dismal 2-12 mark.

After the game, reporters swarmed around Jim Plunkett. It would be their last chance in 1971.

"Plunk, what made you go for broke on that one ... ?"

"Hey, Jim, that was your nineteenth TD pass, better than Namath his first year. What about it . . . ?"

"What are your plans for the off-season . . . ?"

"Going home to California, Jim . . . ?"

The questions came so fast that the tired but happy Plunkett hardly had time to think. He smiled and held up a hand. "One at a time, fellows!" Then the 6-3, 220-pound rookie sensation out of Stanford University proceeded to answer all the questions in a friendly, easygoing manner. It was clear that the reporters liked him. They didn't stay and badger. Once their questions were answered, they left him alone, seeking out the other players in the locker room.

Now Jim Plunkett finally had a moment to himself. His first year in pro football was over. He could hardly believe it. A year ago he had been the most publicized college quarterback since Namath. He had been an All-America who had led his team to victory in the Rose Bowl after setting numerous passing records during his three years at Stanford University. Plunkett's Stanford career was followed by the Heisman Trophy, awarded to college football's top performer, then the wait for the pro draft.

And now his rookie year was over. What a year it had been! A native Californian of Mexican descent, Plunkett was brought east to save the Patriot franchise. And he'd been everything they'd expected ... and more.

He made the Pats respectable. A starter since the first game, big Jim completed 158 of 328 passes for 2,158 yards and 19 touchdowns, the most TD passes for a rookie quarterback since Charlie Conerly threw for 22 scores in 1948. Plunkett was a cinch to be named the AFC's Rookie of the Year. And that was only the beginning. Football people were unanimous in predicting that Jim Plunkett was going to be one of the great ones.

But the Jim Plunkett story doesn't begin with the New England Patriots and a host of touchdown passes. It goes back much further than that.

Jim was born on December 5, 1947, in San Jose, California. He wasn't one of those lucky west coast kids, born into the glamorous California world of bright lights and surfboards. Jim was a Mexican-American. There was something else that made him different, too.

Jim's mother, Carmen, had been blind since she was about 20 years old. His dad, William, was afflicted with progressive blindness. So young Jim had to be an attentive son, and he was very close to both his parents throughout his boyhood.

"We didn't have it all that bad," Jim says now. "My father was a news vendor in San Jose, and my two older sisters and myself chipped in by working after school. I worked at a grocery store for a while, and at various times sold papers and pumped gas. When I was older, I did construction work.

"I don't think we really missed out on any of the important things. We had enough money and enough things to get along. The family was very close and we enjoyed being with each other. None of us really wanted too much, anyhow."

Although his parents spoke Spanish, they taught their children only English, so Jim didn't have any problems when he entered the San Jose school system, where he remained right through high school. He had a lot of friends and got along with most of the boys his age. While Jim is very much aware of the problems many Mexican-Americans have today, he admits he never really felt the sting of prejudice in his school days.

"Maybe I was naive then and didn't realize it," he says, "but I can't honestly say I was a victim of prejudice. I'm aware of the problems that exist for Mexican-Americans today and I'm equally aware of the organizations to help them. I support these groups one hundred per cent."

Unlike many Mexican-Americans, Jim prefers to call himself an American, rather than a Chicano. Still, it's obvious that he has a keen feeling for his heritage. He majored in political science at Stanford and strongly supports groups that encourage and sponsor Mexican-Americans to law schools. He even appeared in an advertisement in *Business Week* Magazine, urging young people of Mexican descent to strive for a career in law. So Jim is using his own career as a means to help others.

It was when he was about ten or eleven that he first started down the road to that career.

"I started playing touch and flag football when I was in the fifth grade," Jim recalls. "We didn't start playing tackle until high school. But I remember seeing my first college game—Stanford against Oregon State—about that same time. And my first pro game was a beaut, the Giant-Colt sudden-death championship game in 1958."

Like most kids his age, Jim liked all sports, but baseball was his first real love and he continued with it right through high school. Not surprisingly, he was a pitcher. The good arm was always there.

"I didn't really start quarterbacking until the eighth grade," explains Jim. "In sixth I was a guard because I was big. I sprained my ankle that year and didn't really do much. The next year I kept growing and was really looking forward to playing when I developed bad knees. Nothing serious. Just something that a lot of fast-growing kids get. The doctor said no contact for a while and that finished football for the year."

The next year, Jim Plunkett made a startling discovery. "I found out I could throw." It was that simple. Jim was in the eighth grade, 5-11, 150 pounds, but he could throw. He immediately became the quarterback at Lee Matheson Junior High and took his team to the county championship.

In his first year at Overfeldt High, Jim was still too young to play on the varsity. But he was busy in other sports, playing baseball and basketball, wrestling, and participating in track. It looked as if Overfeldt had a real all-around athlete in its ranks.

Jim was Overfeldt's quarterback the next year, but again had some knee problems and didn't distinguish himself. Then he transferred to James Lick High for his junior year. By now, he was 6-3 and 215 pounds, as big as many high school tackles. In fact, his coach at James Lick High, Al Cementina, had a little maneuver that he regularly used on opposing teams.

"I used to take Jim with me into the visiting team's dressing room," Cementina says. "Then I'd say, 'Hey, you guys, this is our quarterback. Wait 'til you see our tackles.'"

Tackles or not, Jim was a big, strong, outstanding quarterback. He led the James Lick team to an 8-1 season and the Mt. Hamilton League title his junior year, and came back even better the following fall, spearheading the club through a perfect 9-0 campaign.

Ironically, when Jim played in the North-South high school all-star game that year, the coaches needed his size at defensive end, so he threw only two passes, completing one.

But his regular-season feats as a signal-caller were not going unnoticed. He was approached by several college recruiters his junior year, and many more when he was a senior.

"When I was a junior," Jim says, "I was approached by people from the University of California and Santa Clara. The only eastern school that contacted me was North Carolina, only because the coach had a friend out here who recommended me. I picked Stanford for two reasons. It was close to home and I could be near my parents, plus the school had a great academic reputation. It really wasn't a difficult choice for me."

But it can be a tough decision, and Jim has some advice for youngsters being sought after by a number of schools.

"First of all, the decision must be made by the boy himself," cautions Jim. "If he's lucky, he'll find someone who can steer him in the right direction. But it's got to be someone he can trust and who knows what he's doing. I was fortunate. Al Cementina, my coach at James Lick, was a good friend who always had my interests in mind. He gave me his opinions, but he felt I was capable of making the ultimate decision, and he was right."

Jim came to Stanford feeling on top of the world. He cut an impressive figure, walking down the campus, his husky 6-3 frame held gracefully erect, his high cheekbones and rugged features suggesting a silent, commanding strength. He looked like an athlete. A good one.

But just when Jim was getting ready for the start of freshman football, he received a serious setback. A physical examination revealed a thyroid tumor deep in the left side of his neck.

"It really shook me up," Plunkett recalls. "The doctors told me that if it was cancerous, I could forget football. At that time I couldn't imagine my life without it. I was scared, really scared. At first I said I wouldn't have the operation. I guess I thought if I ignored it, it would go away. But my parents understood the situation and talked me into going through with it. Well, they operated, and fortunately it was benign."

That was good news. But as far as football was concerned the damage had been done. Jim missed the entire training season and the first regular freshman games. When he finally started—he played in the last three games of the season—he just couldn't do anything right. His timing was way off. He couldn't get into the flow of the game and didn't have enough time to work with his teammates. It was a disappointing season and a lost year as far as his football development was concerned.

The following spring, Jim was raring to go. A good spring showing, he figured, and varsity coach John Ralston would have to consider him in the fall. It didn't take long for those ideas to fall by the wayside.

"I really had a poor spring," said Jim. "Nothing seemed to work right. I wasn't throwing the ball as well as I knew I could, and it was obvious that I had a long way to go before I was a capable varsity quarterback. I still thought I could play in the fall, but the quarterback position was jammed up and I really didn't get the opportunity to break into the lineup."

Stanford was operating with three other quarterbacks in Jim's sophomore year. Gene Washington, later an All-American and All-Pro wide receiver, was still listed as a quarterback. So were Chuck Williams and Mark Marquess. Washington was switched to flanker by the time the season opened, but Marquess and Williams were the first two signal-callers. That left little room for the big kid named Plunkett.

"When Coach Ralston told me I wouldn't make the trip to Oregon State for the opener, I was really down," Jim recalls. "I still thought I had a chance to play when the team came back to Stanford, but at that point, I wasn't even an official member of the squad.

"Well, the team came home, all right, and Marquess was the starter against Kansas with Williams backing him up. Later Williams took over as number one. He did a good job, then got hurt against Washington late in the season. Now I thought I'd finally get a chance to play, even though there were just two games left.

"But the coaches talked to me and we all decided that it was silly to throw away a whole year of eligibility so late in the season. That meant I was officially being 'red-shirted.' In other words, while I worked out with the team, I wasn't listed on the roster and technically wasn't a member of the varsity. I'd be a sophomore all over again the next year."

Though he realized by the end of the 1967 season that redshirting was the best idea, Jim was unhappy nevertheless. While not a member of the "I am the greatest" club, he felt that he had the tools to be a good quarterback. Freshman year was disappointing enough, with the neck operation and his admitted poor performance. There was even some talk about sending him back to defensive end.

"I know Jim understood when Stanford redshirted him," said his high school coach, Al Cementina. "When he hadn't played by late in the season he knew it was the best thing. But it was a blow to him. He started doubting himself for a while. But he never groused to John Ralston or to any of the other Stanford coaches."

"The whole thing seemed like a bad dream," Jim says now. "I went to Stanford with such high hopes, and after two years, had nothing to show for it. Football had been awful, my grades weren't as good as I'd hoped, and I wasn't even making friends. I guess all three were related, but it was a definite low point."

Jim returned in the fall of 1968 more determined than ever to make good. Washington was now a permanent wide receiver. Marquess and Williams were gone. The quarterback job was his if he could hold it.

"You could see the difference in the kid immediately," said a veteran newspaperman who covered the Stanford games. "Jim had his confidence and took command right from the start. He was throwing the ball beautifully. He always had the arm and the size. This year you could see he was determined to make it all work for him."

That he was. While Coach Ralston and most Stanford fans expected him to do a good job, they weren't quite ready for the show he put on in the opener against San José State. The game took place on September 21, 1968, at Stanford Stadium, and marked the beginning of Jim Plunkett's college career.

The big quarterback took command right from the opening kickoff. Whether he was handing off to his backs or setting up to pass, he was the boss. When he dropped back to throw, he was a striking figure, peering over his blockers to spot a receiver, then cranking his right arm and delivering a bullet right on the mark. Time and again, he riddled the San José State defenders with pinpoint passes while the Stanford fans squealed with delight. The Indians finally had themselves a real quarterback.

When the gun sounded, Stanford was on top by the unbelievable score of 68-20. Plunkett had filled the airways with ten completions in 13 attempts for a whopping 277 yards and four big touchdowns. The game set the pattern for his performances during the next three seasons.

"I guess Coach Ralston didn't expect to be throwing that much," said Jim. "But he realized that the team would have to rely on passing more than his previous clubs, so he slowly installed a pro-type offense. This helped me in several ways. Instead of having to throw on the run, I became more of a drop-back passer. I was able to achieve more accuracy this way and didn't have to run as much, cutting down on the possibilities of serious injury. It also enabled me to operate in much the same way I would if I decided to play pro ball someday. So many good, roll-out college quarterbacks can never convert to drop-back passers when they enter the pros. I was lucky. I got my pro training at Stanford."

When the books closed on Jim's sophomore season, the Indians had compiled a record of 6-3-1. Jim had shown the way, completing 142 out of 268 passes for 2,156 yards and 14 touchdowns. He had gained more distance through the air in just one season than any other player in the history of the Pacific Eight Conference.

His junior year began with great expectations, and the first game was almost a replay of the season before. Once again opening up against an outgunned San Jose State squad, Jim made it look easy, connecting on 13 of 15 passes for 221 yards and a pair of touchdowns. The final was 63-21, and sportswriters were calling his performance "almost perfect."

Then, two weeks later, Jim was involved in a football game he'll never forget. The Indians were playing the tough Purdue Boilermakers in a battle of highpowered offenses. It was also a battle of quarterbacks. Stanford fans were already calling Plunkett the best in the nation, but the Hoosiers were saying that Purdue passer Mike Phipps was tops. It was hard to choose between them.

Jim was magnificent. His bullet-like passes connected with his receivers with precision. And he was picking them out all over the field, threading the needle between the double-teaming Purdue defenders. Stanford led most of the way ... until the fourth period, when Jim lost a bit of his timing and began missing the mark.

Then Phipps went to work. The Purdue signal-caller had taken a back seat to Plunk's passing all day, but in the final 15 minutes, he was incredible. It seemed as if every pass Phipps threw connected. And, in fact, it did. Phipps put the football in the air 13 times in the fourth quarter, and 13 times he found his mark. When he threw for the final score of the day, it tied the game, and the extra point won the day for the Boilermakers, 36-35.

Fans talked about the game all week long. Plunkett had thrown 46 times, hitting on 23 for 355 yards. His additional 61 yards rushing had cracked the all-time conference record for single-game total offense. Only one thing was wrong. Stanford had lost. And when a guy like Jim Plunkett loses a game, all the statistics in the world don't matter. Jim just went back to work, preparing to meet Stanford's arch-rival USC the following week in Los Angeles.

Once again Jim came out firing, this time before

83,000 fans in the Los Angeles Coliseum. He threw fewer passes, but connected more often, hitting on 25 of 37 for 296 yards and two scores. Still, the tough Trojans gave the Indians a fight for every point. With just seconds remaining, Stanford led, 24-23, but USC was driving. The Indians hung on. When the Trojans had the ball on the Stanford 24, the clock ran out.

But that was just the scoreboard clock! The officials ruled that there was time for one more play. USC elected to try a field goal and sent Ron Ayala out onto the field. With the goalposts at the rear of the end zone it would be a 34-yard effort. The odds were still with the Indians.

The two lines banged together at the snap and Ayala swung his foot into the ball. It was up, long enough ... and *good!* USC had won the game, 26-24. The stunned Stanford bench still couldn't believe it. And another superb Plunkett performance wound up in a heartbreaking defeat.

The rest of the season hardly mattered. Stanford was a winner again with a 7-2-1 mark, and Jim had completed 197 passes in 336 attempts for 2,673 yards and 20 touchdowns. His 113 yards rushing gave him 2,786 yards in total offense. His passing yardage, TD tosses, and total offense all represented new Pacific Eight records. But it didn't erase the heartbreaking losses to Purdue and USC.

"Everything went out of me after the USC game that year," Jim recalls. "The lead changed so many times. I felt joy, then, almost, grief. Finally it just settled in depression."

The losses also brought forth the critics. It's always

easy to criticize a loser, and Stanford was tabbed just that despite another fine season.

"Yeah, Stanford always seems to have the best players, then loses the games," one observer said.

"Especially the big games," said another. "They never win when they have to, when the chips are down."

These comments greatly angered Jim Plunkett. He knew he was simply a victim of great football. Phipps's tremendous fourth-quarter performance and Ayala's powerful kick had beaten the Indians. Not choke-up play on the part of the Stanford team.

"I'd have to say those two losses were a turning point in my football life," said Jim. "I was really tired of people saying we couldn't win the big ones. I promised myself that it wouldn't happen again. We'd beat USC the next time out no matter what. We just had to beat them."

But would there be a next time for Jim? Almost lost in the clamor of Stanford's hectic season was another fact that couldn't be ignored. Because Jim was red-shirted as a sophomore, he had another season of eligibility remaining. But he also had an option. Since his original class was graduating, he could forego his final year and turn pro. He surely had the credentials to go high in the upcoming draft. And waiting for him would be a nice, fat pro contract.

Once again the decision was his. And he made it quickly. He'd stay at Stanford for another year.

"I didn't look upon it as a big deal," Jim says. "The press people made a big fuss about the whole thing, writing about the big contract I'd get and how good I was. But the way I looked at it, I wanted to go back and finish my last year. I knew we had a shot at the Big-8 title and the Rose Bowl. Those things were really on my mind. And I had a few scores to settle. If I could make big money by turning pro after my junior year, I didn't see how another year would matter. The money would still be there.

"Plus there were some other people to consider. All of my coaches and my teammates had been building something for three years. If I left I would always have the feeling that I let them down. We all had a goal we wanted to reach ... together. Besides, we were always telling kids not to drop out, to finish their schooling, to achieve the targets they work for. What would they think if I dropped out to play pro ball?"

Plunkett's decision to pass up the almighty dollar for another year was refreshing. First of all, it takes a rather special young man these days to stick with college when he can sign a multi-year, six-figure contract. Sure, the money would be there the next year. But what if Plunkett sustained a serious, crippling injury in his final year at Stanford? That could happen. Then no money. Just like that. The decision to remain took courage.

If the pros wouldn't have big Jim in 1970, Stanford would. And that meant the Indians would be Pacific Eight contenders and a power nationally. There was no reason to think Plunkett wouldn't be better than ever.

"He knows the game better. I can see that already," said coach Ralston at the outset of the season. "Plus he has the experience and should be able to really move the ball." Offensive line coach Dan Lightfoot agreed. "Sure, Jim's better this year," he said. "For one thing, his pass release has improved. You don't have to protect him forever back there."

Jim, too, analyzed his own game as improved. "I think I've made a lot of improvement in reading defenses," he said. "Playing the pro set has helped. I can make up my mind faster and this gives my receivers a little more of an edge."

This time, Stanford did not open against little San Jose State. Instead, their first opponents were the mighty Razorbacks of Arkansas, and the contest was played before a national television audience.

Plunkett didn't disappoint them.

He came out passing. With a new favorite target in little Randy Vataha, the powerful quarterback hit on 22 of 39 passes for 262 yards and a touchdown. In addition, he connected on eight crucial third-down passes, giving his club key first downs all afternoon. Plus the Indians' first two scores came on last-second audibles at the line of scrimmage. Plunk was reading the defense beautifully.

Most important, the Indians didn't lose this one in the final seconds. They held on to upset the Razorbacks, 34-28, and thus established themselves as a top gridiron power. And it was obvious to all who watched that Jim Plunkett was a more brilliant quarterback than ever.

Two weeks later, Plunk had a poor first half against Oregon, then came back in the second half to engineer touchdown drives the first five times the Indians had the ball. For Plunkett, the result was a 250-yard passing day, three TD tosses, and another score on a 15-yard run. The result for Stanford? A 33-10 victory.

Just when it looked as if Stanford was among the top three teams in the country, the Indians received a comeuppance. Though the Purdue Boilermakers no longer had Phipps, they toppled Stanford from the ranks of the unbeaten, 26-14. The loss hurt, especially since the next game was the big one against USC. Now the Indians would be underdogs to the Trojans. And this was the one Plunkett had vowed he would win.

This time Jim was really on target. He kept finding his two primary receivers, Vataha and Bobby Moore, open and was hitting them with pinpoint passes. He controlled the football and the game. The Stanford defense was equally good. When it was over, Jim had passed for 19 of 31 and 275 yards, and Stanford had a 24-12 victory.

The Indian locker room was a wild scene, players congratulating each other and everyone congratulating Plunkett. The win was Stanford's first over USC since 1957, and now it was beginning to look as if the Indians would be the Pacific Eight team in the Rose Bowl on New Year's Day.

Plunkett continued his outstanding season. He had another big day against Washington State, establishing himself as the all-time NCAA career total offense leader. Characteristically, the play that put him over the top was a 96-yard scoring bomb to Vataha. After the game, Washington State coach Jim Sweeney called Plunkett "the best college football player I've ever seen."

Wins over UCLA, Oregon State, and Washington clinched it. The Indians were Big-8 champs and were headed for the Rose Bowl for the first time since

1952. There was a letdown after that, as Stanford lost its final two games to the Air Force and California. The defeats dropped John Ralston's club in the national rankings, and people began wondering if the Indians would stand a chance in the Rose Bowl against top-ranked and unbeaten Ohio State.

Any team that had Jim Plunkett stood a chance. Plunk finished the regular 1970 season with 191 completions in 358 attempts, good for 2,715 yards and 18 touchdowns. Almost everything he did set some kind of record. Perhaps the greatest marks were NCAA records for the most career-passing yardage, 7,544, and most career total offense, 7,887 yards. His Pacific Eight season and career records fill the book, and he surpassed marks set by such west coast greats as Craig Morton, Terry Baker, Gary Beban, and Bob Berry.

Now all the honors and accolades began pouring in. Even before the Rose Bowl contest, Jim was named winner of both the Heisman Trophy and the Maxwell Award, the two top prizes going to the best collegiate player in the country. He was also given the following honors:

UNITED PRESS INTERNATIONAL PLAYER OF THE YEAR; SPORTING NEWS PLAYER OF THE YEAR; SPORT MAGAZINE COLLEGE PLAYER OF THE YEAR; WALTER CAMP ALL-AMERICA PLAYER OF THE YEAR; AMERICAN COLLEGE FOOTBALL COACHES ASSN. OFFENSIVE PLAYER OF THE YEAR; UNITED PRESS INTERNATIONAL BACK OF THE YEAR; CALIFORNIA STATE ATHLETE OF THE YEAR; and FIRST TEAM ALL-AMERICA ON ALL MAJOR POLLS.

Jim accepted the awards with his usual grace and friendliness. He was already enjoying a reputation as one of the most accessible of athletes, a reputation that continues into his professional career. But the Heisman Trophy, for one, requires a great deal of an athlete's time, and when Jim handed the award over to the 1971 winner, Pat Sullivan, of Auburn, he cautioned Sully about some of the things he'd have to put up with.

"The Heisman winner gets an unbelievable amount of attention," Jim told Sullivan. "No matter where I went, people recognized me. I remember traveling to Maui, one of the smaller Hawaiian Islands, a place where they don't even have television, much less football. 'Now I'll be able to relax,' I thought. Wrong. They recognized me there, too."

"At times, the schedule was hectic. I was flown to New York, then to Connecticut, then back to the west coast. The banquets and dinners can really get to you. Sometimes I ate too much and became very uncomfortable.

"Then there are the questions. Always the same questions. Sometimes I thought I'd go crazy. But most of the people mean well, so it wasn't hard being polite. Pat might have it a bit tougher than I did because he has a wife and child. I was a bachelor, so being on the road and pressured so much didn't matter. I wish him all the luck in the world. He's a fine football player."

Despite the Heisman and the many other honors Jim received at the end of the season, he still had one more goal—to win in the Rose Bowl.

Ohio State was undefeated and boasted a great collection of talent. Coach Woody Hayes had a fine quarterback in Rex Kern, a blockbuster of a runner in John Brockington, and All-Americas all over the place. Jim Stillwagon, Tim Anderson, and Jack Tatum led a stingy defense. The Buckeyes would be tough, and the thrice-beaten Indians were coming off those two end-of-the-season losses.

And there was an old jinx facing the Indians. The last time the Stanford team had been in the Rose Bowl, they took a 40-7 pasting from Illinois.

But when New Year's Day arrived, Jim Plunkett was ready. A record crowd of 103,838 fans jammed the huge Pasadena stadium to see the great Stanford quarterback go against the Buckeye All-Americans.

The Ohio State kickoff was short and Stanford had the ball in fine field position. After a running play gained good yardage, Jim dropped back for his first pass. It was a bull's-eye to Bobby Moore, who carried the ball into the end zone as the fans went wild. Only the ref said no. The red flag indicated that Stanford had lined up with five men in the backfield and the play was called back.

"We wanted to hit them fast," Jim said. "And we did. But when the play was called back we were all a little angry. We knew we had to do it again. To become deflated here could be fatal."

So Jim went right back to work. He drove his club down the field once more. This time there were no long passes, but a steady, ball-control drive. The game stayed basically on the ground, Jim's halfback finally scoring on a short plunge. The conversion was good and the Indians led, 7-0.

Ohio State went nowhere on its first series and

Stanford had the ball again. Once more Plunkett led his team downfield. With the ball inside the 20, he dropped back to pass. Vataha was free in the end zone and the ball was right on target. Touchdown! No—Randy dropped it. This time Stanford settled for a field goal. It was now 10-0 and the noisy throng sensed an upset in the making.

But Woody Hayes's teams don't rattle easily. Quarterback Kern was a magician with the football, and his deceptive handoffs to Brockington and halfback Leo Hayden confused the Indian defenders, and the two big backs began eating up chunks of yardage. Sometimes Kern would fake and carry it himself. Whatever Kern did was working.

This was what the Indians had feared: Ohio State was controlling the ball and the ballgame. Kern marched his team downfield for a score. It was now 10-7. Then he did it again, eating up the clock and rolling over the heart of the Stanford defense. The second touchdown made it 14-10, and the momentum of the game had definitely shifted.

Somehow, the Indian defense tightened when it had to, and by the fourth quarter, the Ohio State lead was still only four points. That's when Plunkett got his second wind. He began filling the airlanes with footballs. Moore and Vataha were taking them from the flanks, and Jim was dumping short ones over the middle to his backs.

When Jim hit Moore on the two, the Indians were knocking on the door. A play later, they scored and went back into the lead. Inspired by Plunkett's passing, the Indian defense continued to play it tough, and Kern could not move his team on the ground.

When he tried to pass, Stanford was ready, intercepting the ball and giving it back to Jim.

This time Plunk looked for Vataha. He found him cutting into the end zone and laid the ball right in his lap. *Touchdown!* The Indians led, 24-14. A pair of late field goals by each club made the final score 27-17.

Stanford had upset the nation's number one team.

There was no question about the player of the game. It had to be Jim Plunkett. Once again he had been the dominating player on the field, completing 20 of 30 passes for 265 yards. His additional 49 yards on the ground dispelled any doubts about his ability to run. Kern, a fine quarterback in his own right, looked like a novice in comparison. Plunkett had proved all over again that he was one of the greatest collegiate quarterbacks of all time.

Sitting among the hundred thousand spectators in the Rose Bowl that New Year's Day in 1971 were many pro scouts and coaches, looking at the various players on the two teams. One, in particular, was very much interested in the performance of Jim Plunkett. He was Johnny Mazur of the New England Patriots. It was the Pats who would make the first decision about Jim's future.

Why the Patriots? Simply because the season before, the team had compiled a dismal 2-12 record, the worst in professional football. The NFL's draft rules are set so as to give the team with the poorest record the first pick of graduating collegians. And it was a foregone conclusion that the first pick would be Jim Plunkett.

But the Patriots had an option. They could trade

away the first choice (e.g., Plunkett) and in return probably get several quality veteran players. That's how valuable a Jim Plunkett was. Mazur and new general manager Upton Bell had already discussed the possibility. In fact, they'd discussed it over and over again. The Pats were in a dilemma.

The original Boston Patriot franchise started in 1960 with the advent of the new American Football League. In the early and middle part of the decade, the Boston team was respectable. They had a good quarterback in Vito "Babe" Parilli, and some top talent. But the team couldn't seem to build past a certain point and had never become a league powerhouse.

In recent years, the Pats had waged a futile battle on two fronts. They had tried to persuade the city of Boston to build them a new stadium, with no success. They had also failed to find a quarterback with any appreciable ability. The team's record grew worse, and the fans stopped coming out. Owner Billy Sullivan finally made some front office changes. He brought in John Mazur as head coach midway through the 1970 season. Then he appointed Upton Bell as his new general manager. Together, the three hoped to rebuild the Patriot franchise.

They got a good start when a new stadium was finally promised. The ballpark would be located in Foxboro, Mass., south of Boston, and would seat 61,000 fans exclusively for football. Since the team was no longer located in Boston, it had to have a new name. First the board of directors voted for the *Bay State* Patriots. That was until Upton Bell came along.

Bell, in his thirties, is the son of former NFL Commissioner Bert Bell. But that didn't make it easy for him. He learned his football the hard way, coming up through the ranks in the Baltimore organization, beginning as an equipment boy and ending up as the Colts' Director of Player Personnel. He knew ballplayers, and he also knew how to sell tickets. One of his first moves was to insist that the name of the team be changed again, this time to the New England Patriots.

"I figured the *New England* tag would give us a broader base of appeal," Bell said. "This way we could be *the* team for everyone from Connecticut through Maine. *Bay State* was too confining. So we had a name and a stadium. Now all we needed was the players to fill it."

That was the key. *Players.* Both Bell and Mazur knew that the right to draft Plunkett could bring the Pats maybe four or five quality ballplayers. It might be worth the exchange. Or it might not.

There was one other factor. Midway through the 1970 campaign, the Patriots had acquired Joe Kapp, the maverick quarterback who almost led the Minnesota Vikings to a Super Bowl victory the year before. Kapp didn't like the way the Viking management was treating him so he jumped the team, winding up with the Pats and getting a big contract.

Could New England afford a pair of high-priced quarterbacks? Maybe the veteran Kapp was enough. Kapp, plus the players they'd get for Plunkett. Injun Joe was quick to give an opinion.

"If you ask me about whether they should draft Plunkett, I'll tell you. When you've got the first draft pick, you take the best player in the country. I've watched Plunkett. He was by far the best I saw."

And Coach Mazur, after witnessing Jim's aerial display in the Rose Bowl, had to concur. "He's the best prospect since Joe Namath. How often does an opportunity like this come along?"

Namath! That was an interesting comparison. Sportswriter Larry Chaflin came right out and drew the analogy. "Not since Joe Namath came into pro football," said Chaflin, "has there been a draft choice who raised as much interest as Plunkett ... Almost every team in pro football is trying to talk the Patriots into trading them the first pick. Billy Sullivan should shut off his phone and not listen to any offers. Plunkett is too valuable to be traded ...

"... For the life of me I cannot imagine the Patriots trading away a quarterback on whom you can build a franchise. In many ways the Patriots are like an expansion team just beginning. They need Plunkett as a foundation upon which to build ...

"... Namath put the New York Jets on the map. He made them a team and he made them financially. Only Namath could have dented the hold the Giants had on New York. Plunkett can do the same thing for the Patriots. He is a bigger name than Namath was when he entered pro football."

Then there were the fans. The Patriots sold only 9,000 season tickets in 1970. Now they had a big, new stadium to fill. The management had to please the paying customers. And the paying customers had some ideas of their own about the Pats' draft choices.

A local Boston paper decided to lend its services to the budding controversy and conducted a "Plunkett

Poll." To draft or not to draft? That's the question it asked its readers. Of the 763 persons questioned, roughly 74 per cent said yes, draft Plunkett and play him. The rest either wanted to draft him, and trade him, or make the trade for seasoned players even before the draft. And some of those questioned had definite strong ideas.

"You'd better tell them to keep him here," one woman said. "I think Mr. Sullivan has pulled enough boners already." Another said, "Why not give the kid a chance? What have we got to lose at this point?" Still another said, "Keep Plunkett, keep Kapp, and trade the rest of the crummy team."

It was obvious that the Patriots' fans couldn't take too many more 2-12 seasons. In fact, they were about fed up already. Many saw Plunkett as a savior, a quarterback who could lead the team back to respectability.

The decision wasn't an easy one. No one doubted Jim's ability. But even hotshot college quarterbacks usually need several years to develop in the pros. Could the Patriots wait that long? They still had Joe Kapp. With the addition of the players they could get for Plunkett, Kapp could make them respectable right away.

On January 28, 1971, part of the question was answered. Football Commissioner Pete Rozelle stepped to the microphone at draft headquarters to announce the NFL's first pick. Speaking in a soft voice, Rozelle said, "The New England Patriots pick Jim Plunkett, quarterback, Stanford."

The suspense was over, at least for the moment. The Pats had Plunkett and now had to decide whether to keep or trade him. But Coach Mazur seemed very pleased, stating that New England had gotten its "money's worth."

As for Jim, the draft news didn't really surprise him. He had been expecting it. "Since I'd grown up on the west coast," Jim said, "I'd be a liar if I didn't say I would have preferred playing there. But I've been resigned to the fact that I would play for the team that picked me."

Later, Plunk added, "I just want to play pro ball. I haven't played in cold weather too much since I am from California, but I'm happy to be with the Patriots. I'm looking forward to being in a new environment and seeing a different way of life."

It wasn't long after that when Jim told another reporter that he knew he wouldn't be traded. "Coach Mazur has told me," he confided, "that they're going to keep me. No trades."

To make things even easier, the veteran Kapp, always a great team player, publicly announced that he would help the rookie in every way he could.

"There won't be a rivalry between us," Joe said, "for the simple reason that every team can use two quarterbacks. Anything we can do to help the club is all right with me. I just want to win and I don't care how we do it . . . or what people are used.

"As soon as I have a chance to talk with Jim, I'll tell him that I'll be behind him 100 per cent whenever he's on the field. And I only ask that he'll do the same for me."

There was still another matter to be cleared up. An important one in this day and age—Jim's contract. Oakland attorney Wayne Hooper was brought in to handle the negotiations, while the local lawyer, Bob Woolf, would be Jim's adviser in Boston. Woolf handled many of the Boston-area athletes, and to keep the pressure off Jim in his rookie year, invited him to live at Woolf's home.

While no one mentioned actual figures, Hooper indicated that Jim's contract would be based on those given O.J. Simpson of Buffalo and Terry Bradshaw of Pittsburgh, the two top draft picks in 1969 and 1970. Both those pacts were also kept secret, but estimated at somewhere around $350,000 or higher. Since Jim and his attorney kept mentioning those two players, it can be assumed that the Patriots at least matched the Bradshaw and Simpson pacts when the papers were finally signed, well ahead of the summer all-star games and the opening of training camp. He was now officially a New England Patriot.

When training camp opened at Amherst, Massachusetts, in July, Jim wasn't there. He was training in Chicago with the College All-Stars for their game against the world champion Colts. But, in truth, Jim wasn't really missed, for the popular Joe Kapp was in town.

Kapp seemed intent on quickly establishing himself as the Pats' field leader for the upcoming season. He wasn't consciously trying to upstage the rookie. But a reporter once described Joe's appearance and demeanor this way: "Joe Kapp looks like an accident trying to find a place to happen." The rough-and-tumble Kapp knew only one way to play the game—all out.

He came to camp in top shape, showing the youngsters and vets alike that he was still a young 34. Off the field, he played no favorites, picking up the tab in bars, visiting players in their rooms, talking about the coming season. Joe Kapp wanted to win this year. It was obvious. He was pulling out all the stops.

Meanwhile Jim trained and played with the All-Stars in a losing effort against the Colts. Most observers agreed that the big rookie showed poise and a fine passing arm, but playing with collegians who had only worked together for a few weeks, he couldn't get any real rhythm or flow going. As usual, the pros won easily, and the collegians quickly departed for their respective teams.

When Jim arrived in Amherst, he received a severe shock. Joe Kapp was gone! Jim couldn't believe it, but it was true. It seems that when Injun Joe signed with the Pats in the middle of the previous season, he hadn't signed the standard NFL player contract. Commissioner Rozelle ruled that he wasn't eligible unless he signed a new pact. Somehow, the details couldn't be worked out, not to the satisfaction of the prideful Kapp. Joe said no—and left the Patriots' camp.

Now Jim was on the spot. He had expected to get some playing time his rookie year. The more the better. But Kapp would be the starter. No one had really doubted that. With Joe gone, the only remaining quarterbacks were Jim and veteran Mike Taliaferro.

Taliaferro was an eight-year pro who had spent the first part of his career understudying Joe Namath in New York. He had been the Pats' number one quarterback in 1969 and had a mediocre season. In 1970, he was awful, and didn't play much after Kapp came.

Now he was in the picture again and vowed to fight Plunkett for the top job.

During Jim's first weeks in camp, Taliaferro ran the number-one offensive unit, while Jim tried to make up for lost time.

"Yes, I've had to cram to catch up," he told reporters. "I feel as if I'm preparing for final exams. I've got to learn the Patriots' plays and terminology. That takes time, although basically it isn't that different from the things we did at Stanford, and it's even more similar to the All-Star camp in Chicago."

Then Jim talked about confidence. "It's natural that quarterbacks carry a degree of authority, but to be completely effective, the quarterback must have the full respect of his team. And that kind of confidence can't be gained from a playbook.

"I didn't really have a reaction when I heard Kapp quit. I only met him briefly. But I felt that I was going to play even with him here. I was confident about that and about myself. I think that one man can give a team a spark, but one man can't turn a team around. It takes the entire squad to do that."

The Pats liked Plunkett's confidence, but Mazur and Bell didn't want to rush him. The early exhibition pattern was for Taliaferro to start, with Plunkett relieving for brief interludes. In the first two encounters with the Vikings and Giants, Jim appeared only briefly, throwing 11 passes, completing five, with two interceptions. He was still learning.

"You could see his poise in that game with the Giants," said Mazur. "We were just up, 20-14, and he was instructed to run out the clock. If he messes up, they get the ball and score. But he didn't. He did the job right."

And Giants coach Alex Webster also admired the youngster's skills. "He'll be around for a long time," Big Red said. "He throws the ball very well and seems to respond well under pressure. That's important."

Mazur brought Plunkett along slowly, though the big rookie continued to receive praise from teammates and the opposition every time he appeared. The handwriting seemed to be on the wall for Taliaferro. He was fighting for his life.

Finally, with the season just two weeks away, Mazur announced that Plunkett would get his first start, in an exhibition against the Atlanta Falcons.

"Sure I like to start," Jim said when asked about his new role. "Wouldn't anybody? But right now I'm still learning and I think I'm doing better every week. It hasn't been that hard picking things up. It's less complex than I expected."

Coach Mazur wanted to see Plunkett in a new role. "Opening a game is different from coming in off the bench," Mazur said. "It's important that we see Jim start now so we'll know what to do when we open the regular season."

The quarterback job was still up for grabs. Mazur made that obvious. In a move perhaps first designed to make Plunkett feel a little more at home, the Patriots signed Randy Vataha as a free agent. Little Randy had been Plunk's primary wide receiver the past season at Stanford. Originally drafted by the Rams, Vataha was judged too small (5-9, 165) for pro standards and released. New England signed him on

Jim's recommendation and before the year was out the move paid dividends.

Jim didn't set the world on fire in the final exhibitions, but he proved he could do as good a job as Taliaferro. That was enough. Taliaferro had been around for eight years. Everyone knew his talents. Plunkett was looking as good and could only improve. It was decided that Jim Plunkett would be the Patriots' starting quarterback in the season's opener against the tough Oakland Raiders on September 19.

Once again the media closed in on the Patriots' rookie signal-caller. Now that he was an announced starter, the pressure was on. In fact, several newsmen reminded him about Terry Bradshaw, asking if he thought the same thing would happen to him.

Bradshaw had been 1970's "can't miss" future star. He was the top draft choice of the Pittsburgh Steelers. Bradshaw was big and fast, with a cannon for an arm, and he had the quickest release since Joe Namath. But after the big pre-season buildup, Bradshaw's rookie year quickly turned into a nightmare.

Terry was given the quarterback job. But when things didn't go right he started pressing. Suddenly nothing would work for him. He lost his confidence. It's said that he often went to his car after the ballgames and wept. By midseason he was sharing the job with holdover Terry Hanratty and the fans were wondering if he'd ever make it.

"I can see how Terry Bradshaw felt frustrated," Jim said. "There are things you did in college and you feel you can do up here, but when you first try them, they just don't work. But I know there are going to be setbacks, and I also know there will be progress.

As long as the frustration doesn't linger on and bother me too much, it's okay.

"That's what happened to Bradshaw. The frustrations just overwhelmed him. He began thinking so much about his performances that he couldn't concentrate on the ballgame. I don't know whether his unfortunate experience will help me or not. Since we're different people with different ballclubs, you can't really compare the situation. But I'll know what to watch out for. By the way, Terry is still going to be a great quarterback."

When 55,405 fans paid their way into Schaefer Stadium to see the Patriots' opener, many of the old Boston faces were back. But there were enough newcomers to give the New England Patriots something of their own identity. The rest they'd have to prove on the field.

In addition to Plunkett, rookie Vataha would be in the starting lineup. Randy had quickly proven himself a gutsy receiver capable of getting open. He worked beautifully with Jim. Those years at Stanford had not been wasted.

Veteran Ron Sellers was at the other wide receiver spot, while rookie Roland Moss got the call at tight end. The setbacks were Carl Garrett and Jim Nance, both outstanding runners on their good days. The offensive line was about the same, but with an additional year's experience.

On defense, the Pats were starting rookies Julius Adams and Tim Kelly, plus new linebacker Steve Kiner, who came over from Dallas. These three, plus more experience for the returning veterans, promised to make the Pat defenders a more rugged crew in the new season.

But no matter how highly rated were the Patriot rookies, no one was prepared for what happened on opening day. In fact, most fans came just to see the new stadium and the new quarterback. As for winning? They expected the Raiders to blow the Patriots all the way back to Boston.

In the first half, Plunkett was playing it safe, trying to get the feel of the game and his teammates. He handed off to Garrett, Nance, and Bob Gladieux, who alternated in the backfield. The few passes he tried were also short tosses to his backs or tight end. It was dull football, but the crowd waited patiently. And they were getting their kicks from the New England defense.

The Pat defenders were harassing the Raiders and their fine quarterback, Daryle Lamonica. Beating the strong Oakland line to the punch, the Patriot front four and linebackers were constantly rushing Lamonica, making him throw early. By halftime, Daryle was frustrated. He hadn't connected on one of his patented long bombs, and it was a short touchdown run by Pete Banasak that gave Oakland a 6-0 lead.

In the locker room, Mazur told his offense to open it up. "They haven't gotten away from us and I don't think they're going to. If we open it up a little, we may take them by surprise."

Some of the Patriot fans expected to see Taliaferro in the second half. But when Plunkett trotted out to the huddle, they cheered.

Minutes later they were cheering again. Plunkett was leading a determined drive downfield. Again it was conservative, but the backs were gaining good yardage, and Jim was beginning to connect on little swing passes to the outside. The Patriots scored on the ground, and Charley Gogolak added the go-ahead point. New England had the lead, 7-6.

If anything would shake up the Raiders, this was it.

Lamonica tried, but he couldn't move the ball again. The Patriot defense was fired up, and they got the ball for Plunkett on his own 30.

Once more, the Patriots began picking up yardage. With a third-down play at the 34, Plunkett faded to pass. He had protection, pumped once, and fired deep. There was little Vataha, grabbing the ball and speeding all the way to the Oakland 27 before he was dropped. Vataha bounced to his feet and suddenly it was last year again, the Stanford combo clicking like old times.

Now the Pats were really high. Two running plays moved the ball to the 20. Then Plunkett faded back once more. A play-action fake drew in the defense and Jim threw to his rookie right end, Roland Moss. Moss gathered in the pass at the 10 and practically walked into the end zone. The Pats led, 14-6, and that's the way it ended. The *new* Patriots had their first win, and Jim Plunkett was an instant hero. New England fans went wild. They had their savior at long last.

For the next week, the Pats stayed sky-high. They had won with their rookie quarterback the first time out. Plunkett completed six of 15 passes in his pro debut, and he hit when it counted. Another victory and they'd have won as many as all last year. And they'd be looking for it the following week against the powerful Detroit Lions.

This time the fans really came out. A record Patriot crowd of 61,057 fans jammed Schaefer Stadium, expecting to see Plunkett & Co. do it again. Instead, they saw just the opposite.

New England couldn't move. The tough Lion defense stopped everything the Pats tried. And the young Patriot defense lost all of the fire it had had the week before.

Jim completed just six of 17 for 113 yards. The only thing the fans had to cheer about was a 61-yard touchdown bomb to Vataha that averted a shutout. But Jim's receivers dropped several other tosses, and Plunk was off the mark with the rest. Detroit rolled, 34-7, and fans began asking: Will the real New England Patriots please stand up?

"It was a bad game, that's all," said Jim. "I wasn't sharp out there. You've got to forget about these games once they're over. The losses you forget quicker than the wins.

"But you've got to be careful when this happens. There is a certain type of mentality associated with a loser. You don't have the same kind of confidence. We can't let this happen because of one loss. We've got to go out there thinking we're going to win. And if we play well and do things right, we will win."

The next two weeks gave the team and its fans a clearer indication of what kind of season it was likely to be. Playing again at Schaefer Stadium, the Pats were humiliated by the world champion Colts, 23-3, then bounced back before another record crowd

(61,357) the following Sunday to wipe out the Namathless New York Jets, 20-0.

No one could blame the Colt loss on Plunkett. Garrett dropped a potential TD pass. Sellers caught another which was brought back for a holding penalty. New England's offensive line withered in the face of the fierce Baltimore rush. Jim was constantly pressured, but didn't panic. He either ran out of trouble or ate the ball. No wild throws into the middle of no man's land. In fact, when it was over, big Bubba Smith, Baltimore's top rusher, called Plunkett's performance "unbelievable."

Even the great John Unitas had kind words for his rookie counterpart. "The boy played a good game," said Unitas in fatherly tones. "Our line was fired up and went after him. But he held up. He's still got some things to learn, like finding his receivers a little faster, but the pressure ... he shouldn't have been under all that pressure."

When a reporter told Jim that Unitas had been impressed by his play, Jim said: "We lost, what does it matter? You never deserve to lose a ballgame. My philosophy is you always deserve to win. If I am one for 20 passing, the running backs have to pick up the slack. That's the meaning of a team. That is winning.

"I admire Unitas, don't get me wrong. But I'm not out to impress him. I'm trying to get every one of the Patriots to accept me and my thinking. Some have it already, like Randy and Steve Kiner, the linebacker. But not some of the others. Not yet."

Plunkett's determination to win was obvious to everyone around him. The Jet game was easy. Namath was recovering from knee surgery and neither of his backup quarterbacks could move the team. But the victory nevertheless gave the Pats renewed faith that they could win. And in the next three weeks, they'd need it.

Going on the road for their first extended trip of the season, the Patriots were poleaxed by Miami, 41-3, and Dallas, 44-21. But it was no disgrace losing to this pair of NFL powerhouses. Then a strong San Francisco team threw them down, 27-10, and the Patriot season was suddenly tailspinning at 2-5.

Jim was down on himself. The big losses were tough to take. John Brodie, the 49er quarterback who preceded Jim at Stanford by a dozen or so years, had some words of encouragement for the youngster.

"Jim Plunkett is great," Brodie said flatly. "But he still has to take over the Patriot offense. He's got to put his personality into it before it will really click.

"But Jim can do everything well. He has no weaknesses that I can see, so he really shouldn't be limited in what he does. Now is the time for him to do what he does best, when he wants to do it."

Maybe Jim learned the lesson. Returning to the friendly confines of Schaefer Stadium, the Pats went on a two-game rampage, whipping the Houston Oilers, 28-20, then topping the Buffalo Bills, 38-33. It was in the Buffalo game that many observers say Jim Plunkett came of age as a pro. It wasn't that all of a sudden he was a perfect quarterback, but he did some little things that you'd expect from a 10-year veteran instead of a rookie.

First of all, he brought his team from behind. Buffalo had early leads of 7-0 and 17-14, but by the half,

Plunk had his club in front, 28-20, and they stayed there.

Statistically, Jim completed nine of 16 passes for 218 yards and four touchdowns, one short of the team record set by Babe Parilli. But impressive as they may be, the stats don't tell the whole story.

On the Pats' first series of plays, Plunkett was nailed hard by several of the big Buffalo linemen. When he got up, Jim felt a shooting pain in the back of his left leg. It was a hamstring pull, a painful one, and in the damp, 39-degree weather, the leg throbbed and stiffened all afternoon. Jim's mobility was hampered severely, and the head-hunting Bills knew it. They pursued the young quarterback doggedly throughout the day.

"Jim showed all of us that he can play hurt," said veteran center Jon Morris. "He never complained about that leg, but we could all tell that it was hurting him. He just hung in there and tossed those four TD passes. You've got to admire that."

The first of the four went to Vataha. It only covered 16 yards but was successful because Plunk waited to the last split second before throwing, even though it meant being creamed by the Buffalo pass rushers.

"Jim loves to play this game," said his friend Vataha. "I knew the leg injury wouldn't stop him. You'd have to drag him off the field bodily before he'd quit. I don't think people realize how strong he is.

"Did you watch him on the one I caught? He knew he was going to get hit, but he waited until I was open. He's the kind of quarterback who can perceive a situation and know what kind of pass to throw.

He did it better than anyone in college and he's learning to do it better than anyone in the pros."

Jim did it again, tossing a ten-yard strike to Tom Beer. His third one was the longest of the day. With the ball on his own 20, Plunkett faded back, saw his primary receiver covered, then ·pump-faked and dumped a swing pass out to halfback Carl Garrett. Garrett sidestepped one tackler, faked around another, and was off to the races, scooting down the sideline to complete an 80-yard, pass-run touchdown play.

The toss to Garrett put the Pats out in front for good, but Plunkett wasn't through. His final scoring toss was a thing of beauty. Again he dropped back. The Bills put the big rush on, but Jim waited as flanker Eric Crabtree cut over the middle. Pumping once, the big quarterback again gave his receiver that extra split second to get open, and as he released the ball, he was buried under an avalanche of Buffalo flesh.

But there was Crabtree, racing into the end zone and pulling the ball into his chest, a 31-yard TD strike. Jim got up slowly. The leg still hurt, but there was a trace of a smile on his rugged face. He got a lot of satisfaction out of that one.

"His improvement has really been something," said Buffalo coach Harvey Johnson after the game. "I remember the exhibition game in Buffalo. He threw too quickly then, hurrying his passes all afternoon. But today I can only describe him as a damned tough kid with a lot of poise.

"He's really learned to control himself in the pocket and is waiting for his receivers to get free. The TD pass to Crabtree was a perfect example. The only way he could have completed it was to wait until the last split second to throw. And he did it, even though he knew he'd get walloped. That was his problem before. He unloaded the ball too soon. But it obviously isn't any more. He proved it to me today."

With the season now nine games old, Jim had the Patriots playing at a 4-5 level. Not bad, considering the team had finished at 2-12 the season before. Sticking with a conservative game, he had thrown just 203 passes, completing 91. But 13 of those were for touchdowns and more important, only eight of his passes had been intercepted. And Jim credited most of his success to the fact that he was playing, a situation that might not have existed if Joe Kapp hadn't jumped the team.

"As soon as I was drafted," Jim admitted, "I knew I wanted to play. Sitting the bench wasn't for me. If Joe Kapp had still been there, I might not have played at all, or very little at the most. I'm glad the situation was more or less resolved when I got to camp. It enabled me to play right away and that's what I wanted to do. And I think it's turned out for the best. I'm learning while playing, and the team is getting used to working with me. But it hasn't been easy and I know it won't be the rest of the year."

Then someone asked Plunkett how he, as a rookie, had established his leadership on a veteran club.

"I just kept doing what I've always done. Step into the huddle and call the play with as much confidence as I can. Plus I always try to maintain an optimistic attitude, on and off the field. Since I am a rookie, I didn't know what to expect from the other teams, and I didn't care. I just remained optimistic, and I always go onto the field thinking we can beat whoever we're up against."

It was a good system, but it didn't always work, especially on the road where the Pats hadn't won all year. Losses to Cleveland (27-7) and Buffalo (27-20) solidified the theory that the Pats were a team still in the stages of rebuilding. They weren't about to pull off any miracle finish. Now it looked as if the club wouldn't even finish at .500. With a 4-7 record, the Patriots returned home for their final game at Schaefer Stadium. And they were meeting the powerful Miami Dolphins, a team that had crushed the Pats, 41-3, earlier in the year. Another record crowd of 61,457 fans came out to bid their team farewell for 1971. And many believed Plunkett and friends could pull off an upset.

Jim wasn't nervous when he stepped onto the field, but he was a little concerned. Two weeks earlier, against the Browns, four of his passes had been intercepted. And after the game, Cleveland's defensive backfield coach, Richie McCabe, told reporters that Jim "has some habits that we picked up and used to our advantage. I told our kids that they could pick these things up during the game and they did."

Patriot coaches weren't sure what the problem was. They thought that Plunk might be watching his primary receiver throughout the entire pattern. Or he might be favoring Vataha too much, especially in tight situations. Now the tough Dolphins would put the youngster to another stern test.

The crowd was on its feet as Charley Gogolak booted the opening kickoff to the Dolphins. Fleet Mercury Morris ran up two steps and caught the ball on his six. Mercury sprinted to his left, avoiding the first wave of Patriot tacklers, then cut up the center of the field with a burst of speed that took him past the second group of Pats. A couple of cat-quick moves and Mercury was out in the clear, racing 94 yards for a score before you could say, "Go Patriots!" Garo Yepremian's kick made it 7-0 and it looked as if the Dolphins would roll over New England again.

When the Pats got the ball, Plunkett came out on the field. As usual, he looked confident. In the first 11 games of the season, Jim always opened conservatively, starting with a running play, and not really opening up his air game until later. That's what the Dolphins expected again.

Morris snapped the ball. Plunkett faked to Nance, then quickly completed a short pass to Vataha on the sideline. Next time he got the ball, Jim promptly threw again ... and again ... and again. Eight times in all. And he was hitting on a variety of sideline, square out, and swing passes. With the ball on the Miami six, Plunk finally called a running play, and Jim Nance carried it into the end zone for the tying touchdown. After one series of plays, Jim Plunkett had already thrown the ball eight times!

The Pats kicked off again. This time there was no big runback. In fact, the Dolphins fumbled, and New England had the ball on the Miami 26.

Plunkett came out again. He took the snap from Morris, dropped straight back, and lobbed a pass toward the corner of the end zone. The speedy Vataha got there just as the ball descended and grabbed it for the score. The Pats led, 14-7. Then a second Miami fumble gave New England the ball again, and this time a Gogolak field goal was the result. With just seven and a half minutes gone, the Pats led, 17-7, and the Schaefer Stadium fans screamed in glee.

The pattern was set. Bob Griese could not move his club against the fired-up Patriot defense, and Plunkett could do no wrong. In the third period he combined with Vataha on a 51-yarder, bringing the ball to the Dolphin 25. On the next play, he went right back to his little receiver for another TD strike. A pair of Gogolak field goals and a Larry Carwell TD interception completed the scoring. The Pats won an astounding 34-13 victory, and Jim had completed 16 of 23 aerials for 223 yards. Vataha was on the receiving end of seven, so it was another great day for the former Stanford duo.

The pair of touchdown passes also hiked Plunkett's total to 17 for the year, second best to Griese in the entire NFL. And while Jim didn't have a shot at Charley Conerly's rookie record of 22, he was clearly in pursuit of the second best total, 18, set by a couple of pretty fair quarterbacks—Joe Namath and Fran Tarkenton. Plus there were still two games left to play.

It didn't happen the next week. In fact, not much of anything happened. The Pats were meeting the Jets in New York. Namath had returned from knee surgery and the press billed the game as a contest between "the king" and "the heir apparent." Neither looked much better than run-of-the-mill.

Namath had a slightly sore arm from his premature return two weeks earlier. So he played it cool. An opening-series drive resulted in a field goal. The Jet defense recovered a fumble for a second half touchdown, and a blocked punt produced another field goal for a total of 13 points. In the second half, Joe Willie handed off 21 times and passed only once.

Plunkett didn't do much better. He scrambled, ran, threw, and in general was rough and unorganized. He threw the ball 31 times and was dumped on four occasions by the brutal Jet defense. He took a tremendous beating and his club lost, 13-6.

Always a great one with the press, Joe Willie was restrained in his praise of the big youngster.

"I can only repeat what I said before the game," said Joe. "He has an awful lot of potential, outstanding potential, and you can see he has a great arm. But as far as reading defenses and doing things right or wrong, I really couldn't tell. We did have a good rush today and great coverage downfield."

Plunkett wasn't nearly as restrained in his admiration for the flamboyant Namath.

"Joe Namath is the best quarterback in the business," he said. "The Jets have confidence in him and that's a big part of the game. He controlled the ball brilliantly and I learned a lot by just watching him. I'll say one thing. He really has magic with that team. They respond so much better to him than to the other guys. When he says, 'Jump,' they say, 'How high?'"

Despite the mediocre performance against the Jets, Plunkett continued to draw a lot of attention. There was just one game left, the one with Baltimore, and the analyses of his rookie season were coming in. Most of them were basically the same. The kid had had a great rookie year, had potential to be even greater, and should be one of the best in the business before he was through. He was a cinch to be named rookie of the year. Then someone came up with another interesting statistic.

Through the first 13 games of the season, Jim Plunkett had been the Patriots' quarterback for every single offensive play from scrimmage. If he played the entire finale against Baltimore, it would be an ironman feat never before accomplished in pro football history. And he did it.

In Boston, the city that still considered the Patriots its personal team, Plunkett was being hailed as a savior, comparable to Ted Williams, Eddie Shore, Bob Cousy, Bobby Orr, and Bill Russell in the other major Boston sports. He'd be the superstar that the Patriots had been seeking since their inception in 1960.

The Colt game served to reinforce everyone's expectations. The final memory of Plunkett as the 1971 season ended was that wonderful long pass to Vataha which finished the Colts and gave the Pats a 6-8 finish, their best mark since 1966. It also gave Plunk 19 touchdown tosses, the second best rookie mark of all time.

Jim threw the ball 328 times as a rookie, not an especially large number of passes for an NFL quarterback, showing that his game was always under control. He completed 158 passes for a .482 completion percentage. His yardage was a respectable 2,158, and he threw for his 19 touchdowns, nine of them going to Vataha. He had only 16 passes intercepted. In addition, he showed he could run with the ball, carrying 46 times for 210 yards and a 4.6 average. It was truly a fine rookie season, maybe one of the best ever for a quarterback.

Coach Mazur said that Jim has "done everything

we expected of him," while his friend and adviser, Bob Woolf, said that Jim was "close to being the biggest representative of the entire Patriot franchise."

Jim evaluated his rookie year with the usual cautious optimism. "I didn't know what to expect when I came into professional football. As a consequence, I didn't know what I could or couldn't do especially as a rookie. At times I thought I was doing a good job, doing good things on the field, things I knew should be done during a ballgame. The coaches showed me the basics, as far as play-calling and defense.

"But there were still times when I felt I wasn't throwing the ball as well as I should. It might have been because of my concentration. It was often split between mechanics, reading defenses, and thinking about the offense. These things should be second nature someday. So overall I'd say that I wish I had done a lot better. I should next year."

So Jim was already preparing for the future. It didn't matter that he won Rookie of the Year honors hands down, or that he and Vataha were both top choices on the NFL's All-Rookie team. He still wanted to do better.

After the season a reporter asked Jim why some great college quarterbacks are successful in the pros while others are not.

"I'll tell you," he said quickly. "You must be able to absorb the beatings without letting them take your concentration off your receivers. You'll see some guys who'll complete 19 of 20 passes in practice, just shooting that ball in there. Then, in a game, they won't complete one. The reason is a 250-pound lineman rushing at your Adam's apple. You get hit in college, too, but not as hard as here."

In 1972, Jim had to put his own philosophy to a test. The Patriots just fell apart. Injuries hurt the club, but in addition many of the young players just stopped developing. Jim didn't have a strong running game or outstanding receivers. Vataha, for example, was injured part of the year and getting worked over by the bump-and-run tactics of defenders. He wasn't nearly as effective as he had been in '71.

It was a disaster. The team won only three games and lost 11. Plunkett was blasted from the pocket time and again, chased and harassed. He took a merciless pounding. One coach even remarked, "He's taking such a severe beating that he may never recover from it."

Jim completed just 169 of 355 passes for 2,196 yards and a 47.6 percentage. He threw just eight TD passes, compared with 19 his rookie year, and was intercepted 25 times. That shows the kind of pressure he was under.

But 1973 brought a new season and a new coach, Chuck Fairbanks, recruited off the campus at Oklahoma University. Fairbanks worked to rebuild the team and restore some of the lost confidence in his quarterback. He was successful on both counts. The Pats rebounded to a 5-9 year. They were even more formidable opponents than the final record indicated. And Jim once again showed the promise of his rookie season.

He had several outstanding games, including a 348-yard day against the Green Bay Packers. He was 18 for 32 that Sunday, with a pair of TD tosses as the

Pats won, 33-28. He had an 18-for-25 day against Philadelphia and went 16 for 27 against Buffalo.

When it ended he was 193 for 376, a 51.3 percentage good for 2,550 yards. He threw for 13 TD's and had 17 picked off. He was still subject to a hard pass rush, but it had to be his best season.

"I felt much better this year," he said. "We all believe in what Coach Fairbanks is doing and feel we'll be a winner in the next year or so."

Thus Jim's situation seems to be on the upswing, with some of the great promise of 1971 returning. The Pats still believe he represents the future for them and should become one of the best. He's got all the tools.

It's been a long trek for Jim since his early years in San Jose. He's traveled some rough roads. Yet this is still only a beginning.

Jim Plunkett is going to be around for a long time.

Roman Gabriel

Roman Gabriel is a big man. When the quarter-back of the Los Angeles Rams stands at the line of scrimmage, he commands respect. At 6-4, 225 pounds, Gabriel is the biggest and strongest of today's signal-callers. As the leader of one of pro football's best teams, big Gabe does everything well. He has a rocket for an arm, runs like a tank, and calls a heady, alert game. And he protects the football better than anyone.

In fact, he is such an imposing figure on the foot-ball field that a former Washington Redskin star, Carl Kammer, once said, "Gabriel is really a defensive tackle who can throw the ball."

Roman has never played defensive tackle, but many of the NFL's monster linemen have tried and failed to dump Gabe off his feet. Pro football fans are used to seeing one, two, three defensive men take their best shots at Gabe only to have him remain standing, like a big oak tree, and getting off his pass.

Just listen to Roman Gabriel talk. He lets you know immediately that he's the guy in charge.

"When you're the quarterback, you've got to have the confidence of everyone on the club ... and that means all forty men. If one guy doesn't respect you, that's the beginning of trouble. It takes a long time to achieve this. But once you have it, you can't let it slip away.

"I remember one summer camp. Some of the veterans were mumbling in the huddle. Finally I just barked at them to shut up. I told them I didn't allow anybody else to talk in the huddle. That's why I always stand outside the huddle for so long. If somebody wants to speak to me, he can then. But when I step into the huddle, I'm the boss. That's it."

Listen again. He lets you know that he's good.

"You always know with me that the ball isn't going to be turned over." (Gabriel has the lowest lifetime interception ratio among the NFL quarterbacks.) "And I don't think you'll find a quarterback in football today who's any smarter in calling plays or reading defenses."

Tune in once more. Roman Gabriel is a proud man, clearly aware of all his special abilities.

"I'm very happy that I'm strong, but I get a little tired of hearing people talk about that and nothing else. As far as I'm concerned, that's a backhanded insult. It makes me feel like some kind of circus freak. It's like Wilt Chamberlain not liking the nickname 'Wilt the Stilt.' I want people to look at my quickness and my flexibility. I think I'm very quick for my size. I work at it. I jump rope, play handball, and do other things to improve my speed and agility. I'm not just trying to pit my strength against another guy's. If I did that I'd be a fool. Flexibility, not strength, is what gets me away from a lineman.

"I also feel that I've got to be in the best shape

physically of all the players. And I've got to be better prepared mentally. So I learn everyone's assignment on each play. If a man, no matter what his position, is unsure of what he is supposed to do on a play, I tell him. If I don't know all these things, I don't deserve being the team leader."

Yes, this is Roman Gabriel. He's been a member of the Los Angeles Rams for ten seasons now. In that time he's thrown 2,990 passes and completed 1,540 for 20,196 yards. He's tossed 142 touchdown passes and had just 97 intercepted in his long career. The Rams have a history of great quarterbacks, Bob Waterfield and Norm Van Brocklin being the most famous, but almost all the team passing records are held by Roman Gabriel.

By now it probably sounds as if Gabriel is on top of the world, an outstanding pro athlete at the peak of his career. What more could he ask for?

But there is another side to Roman Gabriel, one not seen very often. And the candid Gabe is perfectly willing to tell you about it.

"The primary emotion I take into a game is fear. I fear that the club we are going to play could beat me. Then I'm in second place. So I fear my opponent. My philosophy is to live for today. But I can't forget the bad years. They stay with me like scars. There was a time when every win was a big one. Now we win ten, or eleven games a season and it's not enough. So now I'm afraid of losing. I really am."

Gabe's fear of losing is not surprising. In recent years, the Rams have been considered one of football's best teams, if not the best. On several occasions, they've had the best regular-season record, only to lose in the playoffs. There's been no championship flag flying over the Los Angeles Coliseum for a long time. It bugs Gabriel. It bugs the fans. The fans bug Gabriel. They call him a loser.

"There was a time when I played second string on a last-place team," he says, "and no one thought I was very good. Then I become a starter and the league's Most Valuable Player, and people admit I'm good. But we don't win the championship, so ultimately, I'm a loser."

Gabriel has thought about quitting the game on several occasions. He's involved in a number of businesses known as Roman Gabriel Enterprises, so he has no financial need to play the game any more. But he enjoys football. He always has. The game has given him a lot. It helped him overcome a sickly youth. Then it made him an All-American at North Carolina State University. Finally, it was a means for him to overcome a painful shyness and fear of the limelight so that he could fully emerge as a leader of men. It's never been easy for Roman Gabriel.

Roman's early years were spent in Wilmington, North Carolina, where he was born on August 5, 1940.

His father was of Filipino descent and worked on railroad dining cars. Gabe was an only child for twelve years before his brother was born, so he spent much of his childhood alone.

"I had a touch of asthma when I was real young," he recalls. "Sometimes it got pretty bad. I remember having to stop to catch my breath when I was walking to school. Fortunately, I outgrew it."

Young Gabe didn't really have any early encouragement to be an athlete. "My dad and I hung a basket in our backyard when I was still young," he said, "but he wasn't too much of a sports fan. He just wanted me to have it there to play with once in a while. If it became a big thing, he got mad. One time he called me in for supper and I was in the middle of an imaginary game. So I told him to wait till I was through. Well, he waited all right. And he had a strap waiting with him."

Like most boys, it was baseball and basketball first for young Roman. Then when he was about eleven or twelve, he began playing sandlot tackle games with the other boys in the neighborhood. Each team put the biggest kid in the backfield. Gabe didn't play there. He was only 5-5 and 120 pounds. He didn't start really gaining weight until his high school years.

When he got to junior high, Gabe had his first taste of organized football. He played tight end as an eighth grader and switched to quarterback the next year.

"My coach in those days, Bill Billings, wanted me to try out for quarterback in the eighth grade," says Gabe, "but I liked catching the ball more than throwing it and told him I wanted to play end. Then the next year most of our seniors graduated and there was no quarterback. So I volunteered. Oh yes, there was another reason. The team didn't throw much. In fact, I didn't catch one pass the whole season before. So I figured, what the heck, if I wasn't going to catch the ball, I might as well be the guy throwing it."

From there it was on to New Hanover High School in Wilmington. Gabe came in after another pretty fair quarterback had left. His name was Sonny Jurgensen, and Gabe was always being compared with him during his stay at New Hanover.

As a freshman, Gabe was the starting quarterback, but he still hadn't grown and didn't have a great year. Because of a lack of defensive backs, he switched positions as a soph, then came back as second-string signal-caller his junior year. But the team ran the ball most of the time, like Ohio State, Gabe says now; and neither quarterback got much of a chance to throw.

By his senior year, Gabe was almost to his full 6-4 height and already weighed about 210 pounds. Since only three lettermen had come back, his coach, Leon Brogden, had a change of philosophy and let Gabe throw.

"I got to put the ball in the air about twenty times a game that year," Gabe remembers, "and we tied for the conference title but lost the playoff."

As far as colleges were concerned, Gabe had plenty to offer. He played both basketball and baseball in addition to football. In fact, he was the starting center for the New Hanover hoopsters, who won the state title in their division his senior year. On the diamond, he pitched, and played first base and the outfield.

Gabe didn't have a tough time deciding on a school. He wanted to stay close to home and quickly chose North Carolina State. He liked the fact that the football coach, Earle Edwards, reminded him of his high school coach. "Earle was like Leon in one important way," Roman said. "He never put any pressure on me and he taught me to be a gentleman. I liked that."

As for Edwards, he was quite enthusiastic about

having the big youngster in the fold. "Gabe was easy to recruit as far as that goes," Edwards said. "He decided very early that he wanted to come here, so we didn't have any problems.

"I saw him play a few times in high school and was impressed by his strength. He also threw the ball well and handled himself confidently on the field. Plus he was an effective runner, and even then had the special ability to take good care of the football. He threw very few interceptions. Some quarterbacks never develop that last split-second judgment, when to throw the ball, when to hold it back, and when to change the play. Gabe had it and I was glad to have him."

So it was a mutual thing. Roman was happy to be there. He learned quickly that there was more to college than just football.

"The big difference, of course, was being away from your home and family," he says now. "On the field it was competing with four or five players who were as good or better than you. But I realized very soon that football wasn't the only thing at college.

"Actually, it took me almost a whole year to realize I'd have to study. I was like so many hot-shot athletes and thought I could play ball and do nothing else. But you've got to have intelligence to play ball and you've got to have the knowledge for yourself in later life. That was another fine quality in Earle Edwards. He made sure his boys studied and didn't let their grades slip. It was very important to him. He didn't want N.C. State to be another football factory. He wanted to produce well-rounded, educated individuals. And he did."

Roman's advice for high school athletes trying to choose a college is as follows:

"I'd be wary of a school where they just showed you the athletic facilities and nothing else," Gabe says. "Then they're probably just interested in a piece of meat. Make sure you know what kind of academic programs are available to you. I'd also lean toward a place where they don't put the big pressure on you to accept their offer. You've got to make up your own mind and can't do that when someone is always hounding you. And don't visit too many schools. Then you'll be totally confused. Limit your selections before you actually begin going on trips."

As a freshman at N.C. State, big Gabe played three sports—football, basketball, and baseball—and he was no slouch at any of them. Besides being a football All-America at New Hanover High, Gabe had been named conference MVP and playoff MVP in basketball, and all-conference in baseball.

Performing for the Wolfpack frosh on the gridiron, Gabe whipped eight touchdown passes in just five games, fulfilling the promise everyone had predicted for him. Then he stepped onto the basketball court, made the transition from center (where he had played in high school) to guard, and averaged ten points and ten rebounds per game. "I was the sixth man," he says proudly, "and the entire starting five were on basketball scholarships." With the baseball team, he still played three positions, pitching, first base, and the outfield. He also batted cleanup.

When he returned in the fall, he told coach Edwards he was giving up basketball. ("I probably enjoyed it more than the other two, but I needed that break in between seasons.") He'd concentrate on football and baseball, a tandem he continued until graduation.

While several baseball scouts said Gabe had the potential to make the majors, it was on the gridiron that he really showed his stuff.

Gabe was the Wolfpack's leader from the first. But one of the reasons the big soph took over so soon was that coach Edwards had a young, inexperienced team in 1959. In fact, it was a rather weak club, lacking size and depth. Frank Weedon, who became the N.C. State Sports Information Director that year, tells it this way.

"The first two football players I met when I came to State," Weedon recalls, "were Bill Hill and Roman Gabriel. Hill was the team captain and center, all 5-10, 182 pounds of him. And then there's Gabe, the quarterback, towering at 6-4 and weighing about 220 pounds. No wonder this club could only win one game, I thought. Hill and Gabriel were playing the wrong positions! It should have been reversed."

Fortunately, part of Weedon's first impression was wrong. It was true that the Wolfpack had a 1-9 mark that season of 1959, but both players were in the right positions. Hill was captain of the 1960 team and played a tough game at center. Gabriel ... well, he was showing signs of greatness already.

Although injured for three of the Pack's ten games in 1959, Gabe nevertheless threw the football 134 times, completing 81 for 832 yards, and he was ranked first in the nation in completion with .604 per cent. He threw for three scores and tallied four times on the ground.

A more important statistic was his total of seven interceptions. It may not sound impressive at first, but Gabe had virtually no protection from his offensive line, and his passes were sometimes hurried. Yet even as a sophomore, he didn't throw in panic, preferring to eat the ball when his receivers were covered. Since Gabe is a strong runner, the minus 44 yards rushing show you how many times he was thrown while looking for an open man.

"That's something I noticed about Gabe in high school," said coach Edwards, "the way he took care of the football. He's never lost the trait, right into his pro career."

Then Edwards continued talking about his favorite subject. "Another thing I noticed about Roman was his quiet, almost shy manner. Yet he had a lot of self-confidence and was a tough judge of his own performance. He expected a great deal from himself on the field and really worked hard to develop his skills. He was very businesslike during practices and games. He was in command out there and the boys looked up to him right away. But he led by example. He wasn't a real holler guy. That was part of his basic personality and he was always working to make himself come out more. It was a real struggle for him."

Although Gabe found it difficult to live in the limelight, there was one thing he never found too difficult or too time-consuming. That was the kids. Roman never refused an autograph, or lacked the time to chat with a youngster. And it all went back to his own childhood.

"I remember going to Washington to see the Senators play baseball one day," Gabe recalls. "After the game, I tried to get the autograph of one of my favorite pitchers. Here I was, just in grade school, approaching this pitcher that I already idolized. But even before I could ask him to sign my book, he actually pushed me aside with his arm and growled, 'Get out of my way!' Well, I've never forgotten how that made me feel. I said then that if I ever became good enough to have kids want my autograph, I'd never refuse them."

And he didn't. Coach Edwards recalls a pre-season *Meet the Wolfpack* night before Gabe's senior year, when more than 2,000 youngsters lined up to get the star quarterback's signature. Roman was patiently signing all of them until Edwards had to stop it so they could get the scrimmage started.

As far as football was concerned, 1959 was a frustrating year for Gabe. While he was gaining experience at his position, the inept Wolfpack team kept losing. There just wasn't enough talent or experience to do any better. But Roman didn't go to pieces. He continued to play his game and take his lumps. If he had played out of desperation, he would never have completed 60 per cent of his passes.

Then one Saturday afternoon against the University of Maryland, big Gabe really went to work. The offensive line kept the Terps off him that day, at least for the additional seconds he needed to really pick the defense apart. Dropping back with those strong, purposeful strides, Gabe began connecting on short swing passes to his backs, and sideline tosses to his ends. When Maryland adjusted, he'd come back over the middle. On two occasions, Gabe's receivers wound up in the end zone for scores. Unfortunately, the Wolfpack defense wasn't up to the task. The final tally was Maryland 33, N.C. State 28. But the performance by Roman Gabriel had everyone talking.

Gabe had completed 23 of 38 passes for 279 yards and two scores. He set Atlantic Coast Conference records for most total plays, most passes attempted, most completed, and most yards gained passing in a game. It also thrust the big guy into the limelight for the first time in his career, bringing praise from top football people and predictions for a great future.

In fact, Washington Redskin head coach Bill McPeak was in the stands that day, and he called Gabe's aerial show "the greatest single game performance by any college passer I've ever seen."

Unfortunately, there weren't too many headline-grabbing days in 1959. The Wolfpack won only once, a 15-13 triumph over Virginia Tech, and the team looked to next season to rebound. At least, they knew they had themselves a quarterback. But the quarterback wondered if he'd have himself a team.

"The 1959 season made me really appreciate Leon Brogden, my high school coach," Gabe said. "He taught me that winning isn't the only thing. Sure, it's a nice thing, and it opens doors for you. It's good to be known as a winner. But coach Brogden always said that a winner is also a guy who can face and accept losing. Because you're certainly not going to win everything in life. It's sound advice and it made that first season at N.C. State a little easier to take."

If Brogden made the 1959 season easier to take, the Wolfpack team made the 1960 season much easier to take. With more experience, added depth, and some good, new talent, the club had the look of winner from the start. And it was obvious to everyone concerned that Gabriel was going to be better than ever.

In the opener against Virginia Tech, big Gabe filled the airlanes all afternoon, putting his club in front early and keeping it there for a 29-14 victory. The next day, Marty Horne, a columnist for the *Roanoke Times*, wrote, "He (Gabriel) is such a smooth and effective performer that it's a delight to watch him in action. He has All-America stamped all over him. There is virtually no defense for his deliveries. A pro-type passer, he fades back slightly from the quarterback slot, bounces once on his left foot, and cuts loose. His tosses are fast, low, and dead on the mark. His ball-handling leaves little to be desired."

As much as he dreaded it, Gabe was being pushed further and further into the limelight. When he took the field at Riddick Stadium, the fans began chanting immediately, "Throw, Gabriel, Throw," taking their cue from the old song, "Blow, Gabriel, Blow," and an ecstatic Earle Edwards wanted to see even more of the powerful Gabriel arm.

"I want him to throw on first down," Earle said. "I've got great confidence in his passing. Sometimes I wish he wouldn't play it so conservative."

But Gabriel stuck to his guns. "Why should I go for the long one," he answered, "which can be intercepted so easily, when I know we can move with short passes? I can throw long when I have to."

Gabe was doing *something* right. When the Wolfpack came out to meet arch-rival Maryland in the fourth game of the season, they were still unbeaten. Who would have thought it after the horrendous 1959 season? Still, Gabriel and company were underdogs to Tom Nugent's Terrapins and were determined to prove themselves the better team.

Whenever the two traditional rivals square off, anything can happen. In 1960, both Maryland and N.C. State fans remembered the 33-28 encounter the year before. The Terps might have won that one, but it was Gabe who had grabbed the headlines with his record-breaking passing day. Nugent's club had a right to fear the big guy's passing arm. And the word around the College Park campus all week was "Get Gabe."

Shortly after the opening kickoff, it became obvious that this game wouldn't be as wide open as the 1959 contest. Both teams were fired up and playing it hard and tight, the defenses giving ground grudgingly. Maryland finally broke the ice with a field goal, but a 3-0 lead isn't very much with Roman Gabriel around.

The Wolfpack took the kickoff and began driving, Gabe directing the attack cautiously, sticking to the ground and throwing short passes to his backs and ends. With the ball just inside the Maryland 30, Gabe saw an opening. He faded back and looked downfield for wide receiver Johnny Morris, who was streaking toward the end zone.

Ignoring the Maryland rush, Gabe waited until the last second and rocketed the ball at Morris. It reached the receiver well ahead of the desperation leap of a Maryland defender for a score. The kick made it 7-3, N.C. State, and Gabriel had struck again.

"I didn't think he had time to hit Morris," said a reporter at the game. "He seemed to wait too long. But Gabe's arm is so strong that he simply whipped the ball past the defenders and Morris hung onto it. The guy can really throw that thing when he wants to."

The game wasn't over yet. The third quarter was a stalemate, both defenses holding whenever it looked as if a drive was starting. Gabriel was again under tremendous pressure, but he kept his head. With the Wolfpack still in the lead, he didn't want to cough up the football.

Then it happened. Late in the fourth quarter, N.C. State stalled deep in its own territory and went into punt formation. The ball was snapped and the two lines thudded together. The Wolfpack punter stepped into the ball, but Maryland's defensive end was racing toward him and leaping in the air. He got both hands on the kick and batted the ball back toward the goal line.

Now the chase was on, bodies from both teams cascading down on the elusive pigskin. When the referees unstacked the players, a Terp player was clutching the ball in the N.C. State end zone. Maryland had scored a touchdown on a blocked punt! They now led, 10-7, with just minutes remaining in the game. It looked as if the Pack had reached the end of the line.

Maryland kicked off, and N.C. State got a good runback to the 32. But they still had 68 yards standing between them and the go-ahead touchdown. It looked like Gabriel would have to open up now if he was going to do anything.

Terp coach Tom Nugent describes what happened next. "All I can say is few teams recover from a blocked punt so late in a football game. I thought we had them, but didn't count on Gabriel. He just lifted them off the ground. He was walking around shaking his fist at everyone and hollering at them to get out there and go. He wanted to win so badly and he just carried that whole team up the field with him."

Earle Edwards agreed with Nugent. "It was one of the first times Gabe ever became a holler guy. I guess he figured he just had to do it now. I've often seen him dominate a game by himself, but never like he did here."

Gabe brought his team out with fire in his eyes. He barked the play in the huddle and then snapped the club to the line of scrimmage. Extending himself to his full height, he looked at the Maryland defense confidently. Then he went to work.

The drive took just eight plays. On six of those, Gabriel passed or ran himself, and was responsible for gaining 63 of the yards. As always, he didn't panic. Even with time running out he played it cool, not risking a fumble or interception. When he saw his receivers covered, he simply tucked the ball under his strong arm and ran it, knocking over several tacklers before being stopped.

And that's how he finally took it in. With the ball on the 24, Gabe dropped back to pass. He saw Morris covered, sidestepped a Maryland defender and started running. He straight-armed one tackler, then broke into the clear, his long, smooth strides taking him past two more. He was hit on the five, and dragged several tacklers to the two.

On the next play, he simply powered over the goal line for the score. The crowd went wild and Gabe's teammates all mobbed him. North Carolina State had won the game, 13-10, to remain unbeaten, and Roman Gabriel was the man of the hour once more.

The Wolfpack locker room was a wild scene. Laughing, screaming players were congratulating each other and praising Gabe, who sat humbly by his locker, basking in the emotion of the moment.

Most of the players on the N.C. State squad knew that Gabe had a tough time handling too much praise. He went to extremes to avoid taking credit for his own ability. It had to do with his shyness. But during the jubilant victory celebration, fullback Jim D'Antonio couldn't control himself any longer.

"I guess I broke one of the rules we had," D'Antonio recalls. "We all knew about Gabe's humility and rarely told him how good he was because it made him uncomfortable. But that day I couldn't control myself.

"Here the guy is, terrific in every game. I've never seen him when he was anything less than brilliant. But I thought he was especially amazing against Maryland. When it was over, I went up to him and shook his hand. Then I said, 'Gabe, you're the greatest football player I've ever seen.'

"Well, he turned completely red in a second and looked so embarrassed. He just hung his head and looked at the floor for a few moments. Then he finally said, 'Come on, Jim, don't talk like that. I'd be nothing without you guys.' Fat chance."

A week later, N.C. State faced a powerful Duke team in a game billed as deciding the Atlantic Coast Conference title. The Wolfpack hadn't beaten Duke since 1946 and coach Edwards had his boys sky-high for the game.

The hard-fought contest was close all the way. The Duke defense was geared to stop Gabriel and they harassed the big quarterback all afternoon. With the score 17-13 and just minutes remaining, N.C. State began driving. Wolfpack fans were on their feet. It looked like a replay of last week's great victory over Maryland. And with Gabriel at the helm, it could easily happen again.

Once more, Gabe led a calculated drive downfield. He mixed his plays and kept his head. No chance of the big guy fumbling or throwing the ball away. He just didn't do that. With the ball in Duke territory and the clock ticking away, Gabriel faded back to pass. He had all his receivers out. This was it, the go-for-broke play. Gabe spotted one of his ends sprinting for paydirt, cranked his arm and let fly.

The ball was right on the button and the receiver reached for it inside the 10-yard line. He could just walk into the end zone from there. Maybe that's what he was thinking, because he had the ball in his hands ... and just as suddenly dropped it! The N.C. State fans groaned in disbelief, while the Blue Devil rooters thanked their lucky stars. The dropped pass had done it. Duke won, 17-13, and N.C. State had lost its first game and its shot at the conference title.

There was no cheering in the Wolfpack locker room that day. Players sat around in dejection, finding it hard to believe they had lost. One player wept unashamedly. It was the end who had dropped the ball. Then someone was beside him. Gabriel. The big quarterback, himself choked with emotion, put his arm around the man and said, "It was my fault. I threw it too hard. Don't you worry, we'll get these guys next year."

The loss to Duke probably hurt team morale. The Pack rebounded by beating Mississippi Southern, 20-13, but it lost two of its next three to UCLA and Arizona State. The finale with South Carolina wound up in an 8-8 deadlock.

Still, a 6-3-1 record was more than many people had hoped for. The club had been 1-9 the season before, and not many teams can turn it around so fast. In truth, the Pack might have played over its head. Coach Edwards did not have the size, speed, or depth to match most of the better teams in the ACC. But he had a gutsy squad, and he had Roman Gabriel.

For big Gabe, it had been another fine year. Roman threw the ball 186 times and connected on 105 for 1,118 yards and eight touchdowns. His pass completion percentage was an impressive .565, and for the second straight season, he threw just seven interceptions. In addition, he rushed for 174 yards and scored another seven touchdowns on the ground. Most of his totals were new N.C. State records.

After the season, the honors began rolling in. Gabe was named "Player of the Year" in the Atlantic Coast Conference and was picked as "Back of the Week" in the ACC four times. He was twice selected by UPI for the national "Backfield of the Week," and he received the Louis Teague Award as the "Outstanding Athlete of the Carolinas."

He was named to several All-America teams and was one of just four players in major college football to be responsible for more than 50 per cent of his team's total offense. In Gabe's case, the figure was 54 per cent. It was obvious just how much he meant to the team.

Rival coaches also were recognizing the talents of the Wolfpack star. Duke coach Bill Murray said, "Gabriel just stands back there, fakes one way, throws another, and he's great. But it seems that he's at his greatest when the other side has just scored on State. That's when his crowd is the toughest, and that's a real tribute."

"He should be the number one quarterback in all of college football next year," said Peahead Walker of Wake Forest, "if he isn't already."

The words were echoed by Ace Parker, a football Hall-of-Famer and backfield coach at Duke. "Gabriel reminds me of Johnny Unitas," said Parker. "The quickness of his hands and his split-second reactions make him the best college passer I've ever seen."

There was one 1960 honor that football people don't always mention. Gabe was also chosen as a member of the 1960 Academic All-America team. He wasn't kidding when he said there's more to college than football, and his steady B average at State proved it.

When Gabe returned to school for his senior year, it didn't seem as if there were too many more worlds to conquer. He had married the year before and now had a son. Roman lived off campus with his family and didn't really hang around with too many of the players. He still wanted the ACC championship, but the team didn't seem any stronger than the year before. In fact, there were those who said the Pack would be lucky to play .500 ball. And without Gabriel, they might not win a game.

"Gabe was great, all right," coach Edwards said.

"He was easy to coach, got along well with everyone, and was respected by all. I didn't have to worry about him giving up the ball or calling a bad game. That was his strong point. Give me a team of Roman Gabriels and I'd win the national championship easy.

"He and I had just one disagreement, and it ran for three years. Gabe wanted to play defense, and I didn't want to take a chance getting him hurt. There's enough of a risk at quarterback. But he wanted to help the team every way he could. And he thought that included playing defense.

"The funny thing was that he could have been a darned good defensive back. He had the height and the anticipation, and his speed wasn't that bad for a big man. But most of the time we had Tom Dellinger take Gabe's place on defense. He did get in one time against North Carolina in 1960, and wouldn't you know it, he saved the game.

"We were up just 3-0 late in the fourth period and they were driving. Gabe came up to make one goal-line tackle that saved a sure score and a little while later he made a diving, left-handed interception to end another threat. It was a pretty play, and he would have been really sore if someone pulled it on him. But he's quite an athlete."

Unfortunately, Gabe didn't have a team equal to his abilities in 1961. North Carolina State was never known for its football program, and Edwards and his staff couldn't get enough players of Gabe's ability to make the team a contender. In 1960, the Pack started great, winning its first four, and the momentum of winning carried over to the end. In fact, if they'd pulled out the Duke game, who knows how far Gabe would have taken them? But in '61, it all came apart from the beginning.

In the opener, the Wolfpack was edged by Wyoming, 15-14. The next week, an improved North Carolina team avenged its previous loss, 27-22. And after a 21-14 victory over Virginia, State was trounced by a strong Alabama team, 26-7. So the club got off to a 1-3 start and the tempo of the season was set. Not even Roman Gabriel could change it.

When it ended, the club had a 4-6 mark, a mediocre season despite the presence of an All-American quarterback. Even Gabe's stats were affected by the weaknesses of the team. He didn't have exceptional receivers or great protection. Yet he completed 99 of 186 passes and threw just six interceptions. For his entire career at N.C. State, Roman Gabriel threw the football 506 times and had just 20 passes intercepted.

Even with the Wolfpack's sub-.500 season, Gabriel got his due. He was a first team All-America on the Football Coaches Association and *Time* Magazine squads. He was the second-team quarterback on the UPI and NEA teams. The NCAA ranked him as the third leading passer in the country, and he finished fourteenth in the nation in total offense. He set a host of Atlantic Coast Conference and N.C. State records. He passed and ran for 34 career touchdowns and had a three-year completion percentage of .563.

Because of his great size and powerful arm, he was immediately rated the top pro quarterback prospect in the country. It didn't take long for the pros to grab him. Gabe became the number one draft choice of the entire American Football League, as the Oakland Raiders tapped him as their future quarterback. In the older National Football League, the Los Angeles Rams made Gabe their number one choice. Now he faced another big decision.

"When I was a senior at N.C. State," recalls Gabe, "I started thinking seriously about pro ball. I thought it would be nice to go to Washington or New York. That way I'd be able to stay on the east coast where I'd lived all my life. Then two west coast teams drafted me. You know, I was a pretty shy guy and I really was dubious about going cross-country and trying to acclimate myself to a whole new lifestyle. But the Raiders made me the top choice of the whole league, and the Rams traded with the Giants to get the rights to draft me. So I figured they both wanted me pretty badly and decided that I'd have to play in California."

The negotiations didn't take long. The AFL was still in its infancy then and Gabriel decided to go with the established NFL. He signed a two-year, no-cut contract with the Rams, including a sizable bonus, the amount of which was not revealed. Although Gabe signed in the pre-Namath days, the two leagues were already beginning their war, and the amount was probably around $100,000.

"I was happy to see Gabe sign with the Rams," said Earle Edwards. "As soon as he inked the contract, I called up Elroy Hirsch. 'Crazy Legs' was then personnel director of the team and I just wanted to chat with him about Gabe. Anyway, I got so carried away that I told him that within three years he could have the hottest property in professional football."

Roman looked forward to playing with the Rams. The money wasn't the only reason. "The Ram coach at the time," recalls Gabe, "was Bob Waterfield, who had been one of the great quarterbacks in NFL history. He was a great passer and I figured I'd learn a lot from him."

But even before he got to the Rams, Gabe ran into some trouble. He was practicing with the College All-Stars in Chicago under the tutelage of another former quarterback great, Otto Graham. For some reason, the two didn't hit it off, and the opinionated Otto quickly put a stamp on the big quarterback. He said Roman threw the ball too hard, and until he softened up, he'd never be a top passer. As a consequence, Gabe saw little action in the All-Star game and reported to the Rams' camp feeling pretty low.

When he got there, he expected Waterfield to take him under his wing. Disappointment number two. "Waterfield was like me," Roman mused, "a shy, introverted man who said little. But when you're a head coach, you've got to talk. The man didn't say two words to me the first two weeks I was there. Someone told me he believed a guy had it or he didn't, and he expected you to make it on your own. I remember one time ... I guess I was hanging around waiting for him to teach me something. Well, he looks at me and says, 'Stand around and watch.'

"He never taught me anything about the team's plays. During one pre-season game he came up to me and handed me a paper with four plays on it. 'Learn these,' he said, and walked off."

Things went from bad to worse. Sometimes Gabe couldn't even find someone to practice with. 'I practiced by myself. I'd throw the ball, run after it, pick it up, and throw it back again. That was my passing drill."

Waterfield wasn't the entire problem. The Rams had a terrible team when Gabe joined them. There was no team spirit. Rookies came up and tried to beat out the veterans—and got no help from the guys fearful of losing their jobs.

"A big-name rookie like me really got the treatment," Gabe said. "Every time I walked on the field someone would say something like, 'Hey, here he comes. Our savior.'"

When the season started, the Rams proved as hapless in real combat as they had in practice. Waterfield couldn't do anything with them and after eight games resigned in favor of ex-Giant linebacker Harland Svare.

Zeke Bratkowski was the Rams' starting quarterback in 1962, and whenever Gabe went into action, he had the plays called for him. With the team doing so poorly, that was senseless. It was no way for a young signal-caller to learn the game. The Rams finished at 1-12-1 that year, and you can't do much worse than that.

As for Gabe, he was in there long enough to throw 101 passes and complete 57, for a .564 average. He hit on three TD strikes and still had his great ability to avoid interceptions, having just two passes pilfered all year. Many observers thought he had shown enough to rate a full shot the next season.

It didn't happen. In addition to Bratkowski and Gabriel, the Rams had drafted Terry Baker, a southpaw Heisman Trophy winner from Oregon State, and Baker was now being touted as the quarterback of the future. It was hard to believe. Reporters on the scene said Baker didn't have an NFL arm, while Gabriel had an acknowledged cannon. But tall Terry had the reputation of a winner and the Rams were desperate.

No matter which quarterback was on the field, the plays still came in from the bench. That, too, burned Gabe up. "When a new coach comes in he brings a new system," said Roman. "He doesn't know you or what you can do, so there's little chance that you'll be accepted right away. That takes away your chance to build confidence with one guy, and with the Rams in those days, there was a constant changing of personnel. It just wasn't working."

By the season's end, Bratkowski had been traded to Green Bay and Baker had proved what many already knew. He didn't have the arm. That left Gabe to finish the season as number one. The team showed some improvement, winding up at 5-9. Roman's stats showed 130 out of 281 for 1,947 yards and eight touchdowns. His percentage was just .463, but he had thrown more than ever before in his life.

Yet it wasn't enough. Before Gabe could relax and count himself the Rams' top quarterback, word came that the team had drafted Bill Munson, a cool Utah State signal-caller who had been rated one of the ten best college passers of the 1963 season. It would be the same story again next year.

Of course, there are two sides to every tale. Svare was often questioned by the press for his reluctance to simply install Gabriel as his number one. Most observers liked the looks of the big guy and thought he could do the job. But Svare's story was very different. It went like this.

"Gabriel came to the Rams from the All-Star camp," said Harland, "and he couldn't even throw the ball as well as I can. And you know how I throw. The guy couldn't even spiral the ball."

At this point, a reporter said that he had seen Gabe play for N.C. State against UCLA, and that Gabe was magnificent.

"I can't explain it," continued the coach, "but believe me, he couldn't throw a decent spiral. And it just went on and on. Finally, near the end of his rookie year, he came around. We said then that he'd be our starter in '63. But then he came back and couldn't hit his receivers ... for weeks on end. He threw hard, but with no accuracy. It was that way in practice and in the game. He was throwing at about a 37 per cent completion average. And we can't win like that. Then he started coming around again, so we went back to him. If we can keep it up, he'll start again next year. But he's been so erratic that we picked up Munson for insurance."

Gabe tells it differently. "Svare just sat me down my second year," he said. "He tried all the other guys while I sat. And sitting is humiliating. It kills all your desire.

"Sure, I had a lot to learn. I'll admit it. But you can't learn from the sidelines. Guys who say quarterbacks pick up experience on the bench are nuts. It's on the field where you find out what works and what doesn't work. You're going to make mistakes, sure, but you learn by them. I've done it all my life."

Gabe was ready to learn again when the 1964 season came along. Munson was in camp, but Svare indicated that the job belonged to Gabriel as long as he could hold it. That wasn't long. In the second exhibition game, Gabe was sidelined with a knee injury. It wasn't serious enough to require surgery, but it did put him on the shelf until mid-October. By then, Munson was playing and doing well.

In November, Gabe was back on an alternating basis, but at the season's end, Svare indicated that Munson was now considered his top man. Roman did not have a good season. He threw only 143 times, completing just 65 for a .455 percentage. But he connected on nine TD tosses and had an average gain of 8.66 yards.

Still, he was unhappy. The coaches sent in all the plays, and he felt he was no more than a mechanical man out there. In fact, the nickname, "Roman the Robot," was heard with increasing regularity. Then one of the Ram coaches was quoted in a national magazine as saying that Gabe was too dumb to call his own plays. That made it even worse.

Knowledgeable football people had a hard time understanding the Los Angeles situation. Veteran Chicago Bear owner-coach George Halas said that he found it "hard to believe that they have really benched Gabriel. Are they that serious about Munson?"

They were. While Bill didn't have the size, strength, or arm of Gabe, he had shown remarkable poise for a rookie and had produced under fire. The Ram staff honestly felt he deserved a full crack at the top job. The fans and press were crying for a winner. The team had lost too many games in the last few years, and there was an atmosphere of desperation in the front office. None of this helped soothe Gabe's ruffled feelings.

"I began to slowly get the picture my first few years with the Rams," he says now. "In college, I was introverted and quiet. But my teammates respected me and I had no trouble leading them on the field, even if I didn't make a great deal of noise doing it. In the pros, I found that I had to change my personality. In other words, I had to show people my ability by talking about it. At first, when I wasn't playing, I just didn't speak up. But I slowly realized that I had to do some selling before I'd even get a chance to play."

While he might have been discouraged, Gabe never thought about giving up. When he was coming back from a knee injury in 1964, the team physician, Dr. Jules Rasinski, Jr., marveled at his concentration and effort.

"Munson was playing well and Gabe was sidelined with this injury," Dr. Rasinski recalls. "We had him on the knee machine, working his leg up and down to give it strength and restore mobility. Gabe always stayed on the machine longer than was required. He was tireless. He just kept at it. I used to marvel at the character that kept him there and the desire that he had to get back in shape and play."

Then came 1965, one of the pivotal years in Gabe's so-far checkered career. The final stats were 83-173, for 1,321 yards and 11 touchdowns, a passing percentage of .479 with only five interceptions. Not bad. But the numbers indicate that Gabe was an alternate quarterback once again. It's not quite as simple as that.

Munson was number one when the season began

and Gabe's disenchantment increased. He was finally approached by the Oakland Raiders, the AFL team that had drafted him in 1961. The Raiders and their shrewd owner-general manager Al Davis offered Gabe a big contract to jump to their league when his current contract expired. He signed.

Then, in November, Munson suffered a severe knee injury that required surgery. It finished him for the season and reinstated Gabe at the helm. He did well. Showing more poise and some fine clutch passing, he again convinced many experts that he was ready. The only problem was that for some reason, Svare didn't think he could win with Gabriel. So Roman was prepared to jump leagues.

Then, suddenly, Svare was gone, and a man named George Allen was appointed the new Ram coach. Allen was an assistant to George Halas at Chicago, and Papa Bear considered him so vital to the Chicago organization that he went to court to keep Allen in the Windy City. The ploy failed and George came to L.A. One of the first things he did was look up Gabriel.

"I hear you're thinking of playing for the Raiders," he said to Gabe. "Well, I just want to tell you that I plan to change a lot of things around here. We're going to be a winning team from now on and I want you as my quarterback."

Roman took one look at the team's fiery new leader and believed him. In any case, Munson's slow recovery from his operation had been further complicated by a toe fracture and a series of virus attacks that pretty much left the job open for Gabe. He decided to stay with the Rams.

It didn't take Allen long to work his magic on the rest of the team. In the previous several years, the Rams had acquired some fine individual ballplayers, especially on the defensive unit, and Allen quickly had them thinking less of themselves and more of the team. He reminded them of their pride, something long forgotten. Even Gabe realized that this had been a problem.

"I couldn't believe the emotional change in the Rams immediately after coach Allen came. Everyone started working harder and making sacrifices, something that had never been done before. But they were enjoying it. Suddenly the team had pride again. That's the first thing losers lose, their pride. Even those guys making big money. We were 4-10 and in last place in 1965. But when 1966 started, we thought we could win."

And with that key word—win—began the second phase of Roman Gabriel's professional career. After four years of frustration and humiliation, Gabe was a starting quarterback and he was a winner.

The Rams didn't become champions overnight. There were still holes to fill and a new system to install. But Allen was in command and he had an able lieutenant in Gabriel. Though once again, Gabe more or less took a back seat—this time to the defense.

That was the first unit to really mesh. With a mammoth front wall composed of David "Deacon" Jones, Merlin Olsen, Roger Brown, and Lamar Lundy—the famed "Fearsome Foursome"—Ram defenders began to terrorize opposing teams and Coliseum fans roared every time these four behemoths trod onto the field. Allen quickly had one of the best units in pro ball.

Meanwhile Gabriel was taking over the offense. He had a good runner in Dick Bass and fine receivers in Bernie Casey and Jack Snow, plus a better-than-average offensive line. If there was one thing the team lacked, it was breakaway speed, both in the backfield and at end. That's a problem the Rams failed to solve, even during their big years.

But Gabe knew how to work with the material available. Running the team with new-found assurance, Roman led the Rams to an 8-6 year in 1966. True, the team still trailed Green Bay and Baltimore in the NFL's Western Division, but the former doormats of the league had scored 289 points while holding the opposition to just 212.

As for Roman, his first year as starting quarterback produced some all-time highs. He threw the ball 397 times, completing a team record 217 passes for 2,540 yards. Ten of his tosses went for touchdowns. However, he also had a career high of 16 intercepts, proof that he was still learning his craft.

Many people predicted that the Rams would be serious title contenders in 1967. However, before they could make a run at a title that had eluded them since 1955, the Rams had to settle some internal crises. And once again Roman Gabriel was involved.

The first crisis was an old story, with a reverse twist. Since Gabe had supplanted Bill Munson, Bill was edgy. His injuries were healed and he wanted to play. When Allen indicated he was going to stick with Gabriel, Munson went into the old "play me or trade me" routine. He was traded, to Detroit, and big Gabe finally had a steady job. It didn't take him long to seek some workman's compensation.

In May of 1967, Gabe announced through his lawyer, Edward Masry, that he had a valid contract with the Oakland Raiders of the American Football League. Roman had signed that pact earlier and it called for an estimated $400,000. But after signing, Allen had persuaded his quarterback to sign a new contract with the Rams that ran through 1967. Since the two leagues had completed a merger, NFL Commissioner Pete Rozelle ruled that Gabe had to stay with the Rams.

To counter that move, Gabriel filed a $200,000 lawsuit against the Raiders, the Rams, and the National and American football leagues. The amount was the difference between his contract with the Raiders and his pay from the Rams. The lawsuit charged the leagues with violating the anti-trust laws by merging. It was an embarrassing situation for all concerned, but Gabe felt he was doing the right thing, since the futures of many pro football players were at stake.

Gabriel's complaint further charged that after the merger, the Raiders had taken the position that the contract was rescinded and they had no further obligation to him. But he still claimed he was "ready, willing, and able to play for the Raiders this year." Now, with Rozelle's decision, Gabe said he'd continue to play for the Rams to the best of his ability. He really wanted the right to make his own choice. If that wasn't possible, however, he wanted compensation.

The lawsuit stayed in the headlines for a few weeks, then was suddenly dropped. Gabe signed a new, long-term contract with the Rams that was more to his liking. After treating him like an unwelcome guest for five years, the Rams now wanted to be sure that Gabriel was happy and had found a home.

It proved a wise move. With the Western Conference split into two divisions in '67, the Rams really poured it on, engaging in a neck-and-neck battle with Baltimore all season long. In the fifth game of the year, the two giants battled to a 24-24 tie. Other than that, both kept winning. Near the season's end, the Rams trailed Baltimore by a game, one defeat to none, both having played to a pair of ties. And they'd meet once more in the season finale.

But Los Angeles had a big one first. They'd meet the powerful Packers, who were en route to the Central Division title in the Western Conference. There was a tremendous crowd on hand in the Coliseum to witness the clash. The Rams started fast and led at halftime, but Bart Starr rallied his team and brought them the lead, 24-20, with only minutes left in the fourth period. It looked like a great season might end right here, because if they lost, it wouldn't matter who won the game with Baltimore.

Then the Rams got a break. Green Bay was forced to punt and L.A.'s Tony Guillory burst through a hole in the line and blocked it. The Rams had one last chance. Calmly, Gabriel took charge. He ran a few plays to set things up. Then he faded back to pass, peered out at his receivers, and let fly in the direction of veteran Bernie Casey. Casey beat his man and grabbed the ball as he sprinted into the end zone. The Rams had done it.

"I'll never forget the cheers coming down from the fans," Gabe recalls. "And the emotion expressed by our players was unbelievable. We felt a love, a relief, a joy that was indescribable. We hugged one another and many of us cried."

There was still one more to go. Now Gabe would be facing his longtime idol, John Unitas, still considered the master by most football people. And Johnny U. was having a big year, as his club's 11-0-2 record indicated. But on a warm December day in Los Angeles, he met his match in big Roman Gabriel.

All afternoon, Gabe directed an almost flawless attack. He picked his plays with precision, mixing his running and passing to fool the fine Baltimore defense. And when he went to the air he was rarely off target. Gabe had a field day and the outcome was never in doubt. He completed 19 of 31 passes for 297 yards and three touchdowns. Los Angeles won the game, 34-10, and the Coastal Division championship with an 11-1-2 record. Gabriel and the Ram offense produced 398 points, and the defense yielded just 196.

For Roman, the 1967 season was a great one. He had thrown for 2,779 yards and a career high of 25 touchdowns. After just two years as a starter, many were already calling him the best quarterback in the game.

But it wasn't over. With the new divisional set-up, the Rams had to play the Packers again for the Western Conference title. And if they got by that one, they'd play the Eastern Conference winner for the NFL championship and the right to go to the Super Bowl. Allen drilled his team hard for the Packer clash. Green Bay had won the first Super Bowl the year before and had been the dominant team for five years. Now they were aging, and many said 1967 would be their last stand under their great coach Vince Lombardi. The Packers rarely lost a big game.

On December 23rd, the two teams met at Milwaukee County Stadium under snowy, 20-degree skies. And it was getting colder. Packer weather. For most of the first quarter, neither team moved the ball. Then with 4:31 left, the Packers started driving. They moved from their own 13 to the 43. Starr faded back and hit Carroll Dale for a nine-yard gain, but Dale fumbled when hit and Chuck Lamson recovered for the Rams on the L.A. 48.

Now it was Gabe's turn. Halfback Les Josephson gained five yards and a facemask penalty tacked on 15 more to the Packer 32. After Dick Bass gained three to the 29, Gabe faded back to pass. He looked for Casey and found him racing down the left sideline. The pass was perfect and Bernie toted it to paydirt for a score. Bruce Gossett's kick made it 7-0 with the first quarter coming to an end. Now if the Rams could only keep the momentum!

They couldn't. Midway through the second period, the Pack received a punt at its own 46. On the next play, speedy Travis Williams bolted through the right side of the Ram line and raced 54 yards to the end zone. The point made it a 7-7 game.

The Rams were stopped again by the aroused Packer defense, and Starr went back to work. With just 47 seconds remaining in the half, bad Bart tossed a 17-yard scoring strike to Dale and the Pack led, 14-7.

That did it. An 80-yard march in the third period made it 21-7, and a 73-yard drive in the fourth ended it all at 28-7. The Rams couldn't get untracked. Their long season was over.

Gabe didn't have a good day. He was just 11 for 31, compared to Starr's fantastic 17 for 23. But once the Rams got behind, he was forced to throw more and the Packer defense wouldn't allow it.

"We just weren't ready," Roman said later. "We had never played there before and we used ourselves up getting there. We just got beat. I didn't like it, but I could live with it. I knew I wanted to be back there again."

It took two years to accomplish that. Though the Rams put together another fine season in 1968, finishing at 10-3-1, the Colts were that much better, having an outstanding 13-1 year. So Allen and Gabriel vowed to do it all in '69.

The team started out as if it were untouchable. The Rams took to the gridiron eleven times and came off winners eleven times. Gabe was playing better than ever, enjoying his finest season. He looked like the complete quarterback, an inspirational leader and pinpoint passer. When L.A. won its eleventh straight there was talk of an undefeated season. Baltimore had slipped and the Rams were already the Coastal Division champs.

"That's what hurts us," Gabe says now. "We won our division so early that we suffered a letdown."

The letdown came in the form of three straight losses. But nevertheless the Rams were division winners once more and would have another crack at the title. This time they'd meet the Central Division powerhouse Minnesota Vikings, who finished their year at 12-2.

The Ram balance changed in '69. Till then, the defense had always seemed to be the heart of the team. But the veterans were getting old and now the offense became the team's strong point. Ironically, it was the Vikings who were the premier defensive team, featuring a front four known as the "Purple People Eaters," four All-Star linemen who many said were even superior to the "Fearsome Foursome."

There was another reason fans looked to the title game as the big one. Before it took place, Gabe was named the NFL's Player of the Year, beating out the Vikings' rough-and-tumble quarterback, Joe Kapp, for that honor. It was one of the high points of Gabe's career. There wasn't anyone who doubted his ability now. He had just finished a season with 217 completions in 399 attempts for 2,549 yards and 24 touchdowns. What's more, he had just seven passes intercepted. That's only one every two games, an amazing tribute to his accuracy and judgment.

But none of that mattered when the Rams met the Vikings at Metropolitan Stadium in Minneapolis. The sky was overcast and the temperature down around the 20-degree mark.

This time the Rams were ready. In the first period, Carl Eller intercepted a Gabriel screen and returned it for an apparent touchdown. But Alan Page was offside and the play came back. Gabe didn't let it bother him. Given a second chance, he marched his team downfield and completed a little roll-out to Bob Klein from three yards out for the score. The drive covered 45 yards in eight plays.

After the Vikings tied it with a long march of their own, Gossett kicked a 20-yard field goal to put L.A.

back on top. The Vikings couldn't move and punted. An 11-yard return by Alvin Haymond put the ball on the Ram 44. Roman quickly got down to cases. He hit tight end Billy Truax for a 16-yard gain, then went right back to him for 18 more. Larry Smith and Josephson took turns carrying the ball down to the two, and Gabe used the little roll-out pass to Truax in the end zone for another score. At the half it was 17-7 and looking like the Rams might have that title after all.

But the Vikes were a never-say-die club, and in the cold twilight of Metropolitan Stadium, they began to rally. Kapp hit on a 41-yard bomb to Gene Washington at the beginning of period three, bringing the ball to the L.A. six. Three plays later, Dave Osborne went over and it was a 17-14 ballgame. Meanwhile the front four, Eller, Page, Gary Larsen, and Jim Marshall, were making mincemeat of the Ram offensive line and getting to Gabriel, forcing him to eat the ball on several occasions, and hurrying his passes on others. Roman didn't have time to throw long and was hitting on short screens and square-outs. It wasn't enough to move the team.

At the outset of the final period, Gabe engineered a drive that ended with a Gossett field goal from the 27. The score was now 20-14 with 14 minutes to play.

The Ram defense dug in, but it couldn't stop the determined Vikings. Kapp threw to John Henderson for 20, then to fullback Bill Brown for 12. The Vikes had a second-down play at the Ram 16, when Kapp took off around left end and bullied his way to the four. Two plays later, Injun Joe carried it in from the two and put his team in front for the first time, 21-20.

Los Angeles got the kickoff at the 12 and Gabe came out hoping to pull off another rally. But on the first play from scrimmage, Eller burst through a gaping hole and bear-hugged Gabe at the goal line. They fell into the end zone for a safety and the Vikings had two more points and the ball. It was 23-20.

With one more chance, Roman moved the ball from his own 15 to the Viking 44, hitting on seven straight passes, most of them short sideline tosses designed to stop the clock. With a first down at the 45, he hit Josephson for a gain of one. Time was running out. He went to his dependable tight end, Truax, but a Viking linebacker was there to bat it away. Only 39 seconds left.

Gabe faded again and threw over the middle. There was big Alan Page, grabbing the ball in a huge paw and lugging it 29 yards upfield before Gabriel himself made the tackle.

All Kapp had to do was run out the clock and it was over. For the second time in three years the Los Angeles Rams had lost the big game, bowing to the Super Bowl-bound Vikings, 23-20. A deep gloom settled over the Ram locker room.

"I can't say we weren't ready for this one," Gabe admitted. "We played a good first half, but they had a tremendous second half to beat us.

"You know, I'll never forget Page's interception. We had a good drive going and I thought we were going to pull it out. But there was a breakdown in the play and no one was there but Page. I just sat in the dressing room and thought about all those days and weeks and months of work and sacrifice. All the games, all the wins. And now . . . nothing. I was crushed and I cried. Nothing anyone said could help. I doubt if most people reach that same kind of emotional letdown in their lives. I felt I'd let the team down. I felt emptiness. I wanted to quit."

Gabe's feelings were understandable. He had reached the top of his profession, yet had failed to achieve the one thing that's deemed most important—the championship. It's also the one standard upon which so many people ultimately judge success and failure in sports. For all his accomplishments, they started calling him a loser.

"Why didn't I quit?" Gabe said later. "I guess because time heals most wounds. I still wanted the championship for the Rams and I knew I was an important part of a great team. I also felt I was at my peak as a player, so I came back with absolutely no regrets."

But the Gabriel òdyssey doesn't end here. As always, Roman was steeped in some sort of controversy or another. He was no longer the shy kid from Wilmington, North Carolina. He spoke his mind freely on any and all subjects. After the 1969 season, Ram owner Dan Reeves abruptly fired George Allen, saying that the coach refused to communicate with him on matters directly affecting the team. Gabriel led a group of Ram veterans who publicly announced they'd quit, too, if Allen left. Reeves knew a guy like Gabe wasn't fooling, and reinstated the coach for the duration of his contract.

Perhaps that was one of the reasons the team tailed off slightly in 1970, finishing second to the San Francisco 49ers in the race for the divisional title. Gabe had another good year, but many thought the Rams

were starting to fade, having reached their peak in
'69.

After the year ended, Allen left, taking over at
Washington, where he immediately started all over
again in trying to transform a loser to a winner. He
did the same things he had done in Los Angeles, pro-
claiming "the future is now," and trading away draft
choices for proven veterans. Eight of those veterans
came from the Rams, and for a while it was rumored
that Gabriel would soon join his ex-coach. Gabe still
had bad memories of coaching changes from his early
pro years.

But Roman was now firmly rooted in California. He
had several business ventures with teammate Merlin
Oslen and had formed his own company, Roman Gabriel Enterprises. Soon after the rumors started, Gabe
dispelled them by signing a new contract, calling for
upwards of $100,000 a season and making him one of
the highest-paid quarterbacks this side of Joe Namath.

Once that matter was settled, Gabe again let it be
known that he was a Ram forever. In fact, he and Allen even exchanged some verbal insults resulting from
the rumors that Gabe would go to Washington.

Roman had a sub-par year in 1971, sub-par for him,
that is. He completed just 180 of 352 passes, and his
yardage total was the lowest since 1964. The team
was beset by injuries from the first, and again finished
second to San Francisco. Still no championship.
Though Gabriel already holds almost all the Ram
passing records, he goes on, looking to improve his
game and still searching for that big one.

Many fans thought he'd be discouraged after 1971.

The team didn't bounce back under Tommy Prothro, who had come from UCLA to replace Allen. The Rams may be facing a rebuilding stage before being serious contenders again. But Gabe still has the desire to play.

"When I heard that the 49ers beat Detroit to clinch the Coastal title, I was ready to play some more football right then," he said recently. "I think the Rams are still a top team and can go all the way. We had some new personnel last season and that usually takes a year to iron itself out. The coach was new. Lance Rentzel, a great receiver, was new; and some of our defensive people were new. So I'm optimistic."

Gabriel has always been known as the strongest and most durable quarterback in the game. But he's had his hurts. "I've had four knee operations now, an elbow operation, a broken nose, and the usual bumps and bruises. It seems as if I'm having something done after every season. But I've learned it's best to keep the injuries to myself. If you publicize them, the head-hunters will come after you."

Nevertheless, football has been good to Roman Gabriel. It's enabled him to mature as a person, and to come out of the shell of shyness that had enveloped him for so many years. He's a well-known personality now, having hosted a TV show, starred in a movie with John Wayne, and appeared in several television series. He wears his hair longer now, and his rugged good looks are familiar to anyone who follows professional football.

Things can change quickly in the pro game. At the end of 1970 Roman had said he was a Ram forever. Yet when 1972 began, the promise of a comeback year was quickly diminished. In training camp Gabe suffered a collapsed lung. That put him on the shelf for almost a month. He made a good recovery and began getting in shape. Then his arm started hurting. He had tendonitis of the elbow.

Word was that Gabe couldn't throw long and the defenses played it that way. There were other problems with the Rams that year, but when the club failed to win big games, Gabe got the blame.

"There's nothing wrong with me," he insisted. "I'm not going to make any excuses for my play."

That was typical Gabriel. But after the season it was revealed that he had again played in tremendous pain, even trying acupuncture treatments on the arm. The club finished a disappointing 6-7-1, and missed the playoffs. Statistically, Gabe's season wasn't bad, that is for most quarterbacks, though he normally did much better.

He completed 165 of 323 passes for 2,027 yards and a 51.1 percentage. But he only threw for 12 TD's and had 15 intercepted. Those certainly weren't Gabriel norms.

The Rams made a coaching change in the off-season, bringing in Chuck Knox, who had been an assistant in Detroit. Then there was another change. Quarterback John Hadl was acquired from San Diego. Observers figured that he'd compete with Gabe for number one.

"Roman and I are good friends," said Hadl. "I don't think we'll have any problems. We both know what we have to do."

Gabe liked Hadl, but wasn't happy with the situation. He felt the Rams had lost confidence in him and didn't want to battle for a job like an untried rookie.

"It won't work," he said, shortly after the Hadl deal. "I guess my days in Los Angeles have come to an end. I won't play under these circumstances; I want to be traded."

So he got his wish. The Rams shipped Gabe to the Philadelphia Eagles, one of the weakest teams in the league. Many observers thought Gabe would balk. All his business interests were on the west coast and he was going to an acknowledged loser. Some thought he'd quit. Not Gabe. Not at age 33.

Feeling that he had something to prove, he looked forward to playing in Philly. The Eagles were rebuilding under new coach Mike McCormack and a whole new staff. The club had given up all-pro wide receiver Harold Jackson, runner Tony Baker, and three draft choices for Gabe. They wanted him.

"Gabe gives us the poise and leadership a young team needs," said McCormack. "With him at the controls I think we can compete with anyone."

That was Gabe's attitude, as well. He took charge immediately, and quickly dispelled rumors that there was anything wrong with his arm. He made Philly the passingest team in the league, and put together one of the greatest seasons of any quarterback ever.

"The Eagles were the worst offensive team in the league in '72 and won just two games," said team PR man Chick McElrone. "Roman made us the best passing club and second best offensive team overall."

There was the old Gabriel clutch play again. Against St. Louis he calmly flipped a 24-yard TD pass to Don Zimmerman as the gun was sounding and gave his club a 27-24 win. He did things like that all year.

When it ended, the Eagles were 5-8-1, and just as easily could have been 8-5-1. That's how close they came in several games and how competitive they were with Gabe in charge.

Overall, he led the NFL with 270 completions in 460 attempts. His passing yardage of 3,219 also led the league, and his 23 TD tosses tied Roger Staubach in that department. He completed an amazing 58.7 percent of his passing, amazing because he threw so often and defenders knew it was coming, and he was intercepted just 12 times.

"Gabe surpassed every expectation we had when we traded for him," said Coach McCormack. "We wanted a team leader and he became an extraordinary one, the hardest worker from training camp to the final gun. He has just done an outstanding job for the Eagles both on and off the field."

So Gabe showed a lot of people that he still had it. It's not easy for a veteran to make the kind of transition that he did, but Roman showed no strain, needed no period of adjustment, and was no prima donna, not for a second. He's starting a whole new career in Philly. His goal with the Rams was always to win a championship. He still has that goal, transferred to Philly. Gabe's a determined guy. He's never ducked a challenge in his life.

And he certainly won't quit now.

Greg Landry

They call it the Yankee Conference, but very few sports fans outside of New England have heard of it. You won't find Maine, New Hampshire, Massachusetts, Connecticut, Rhode Island, or Vermont ever going to the Rose Bowl. They generally stick to their own little corner of the country. There they play before local fans every bit as enthusiastic as those of the Southeastern Conference, Big Ten, or Pacific Eight.

But that's where the resemblance ends. The Yankee Conference schools don't recruit like the big-timers and surely don't attract nationally ranked talent, let alone players hoping for a pro career.

Sure, the scouts get up there from time to time, hoping to find a sleeper in the hills of New Hampshire or the snows of Vermont. If they see a big, brawny kid who looks like he wants to play ball they put him on their lists. But only a handful of Yankee Conference players have been picked high by the pros, and even fewer have made it to the NFL to stay.

A Yankee Conference player being a top draft choice is almost inconceivable, and that player being a quarterback ... well ... that's like saying a jockey could make a good defensive tackle. It just doesn't work.

But who's to say it *can't* happen. Certainly not Greg Landry. It happened to him.

Landry was toiling for the University of Massachusetts in 1967, setting the Yankee Conference on fire with his own brand of hard running and strong passing. A year later, he called the first signal in the opening game of the 1968 NFL season. And he was wearing the uniform of the Detroit Lions!

It's not really as simple as it sounds. There were some highly touted players available that year, including a Heisman Trophy-winning quarterback. The Lions shocked the football world when they opted for Landry as their number one, the 11th player picked of the thousands of eligible collegians.

We'll get to the details of the draft later. Suffice to say now that there was prejudice involved, prejudice against the Yankee Conference. Some people couldn't believe that a quarterback from a Yankee Conference School could be good enough to risk a top choice.

Yet Greg Landry came to the pros, a big, strong, fast, undisciplined signal-caller who liked to run as much as pass. It didn't take long to realize that Greg wasn't about to become a classic dropback passer in the John Unitas–Sonny Jurgensen tradition. He was something else. For a while the Lions tried to change him. It didn't work. Then, when they decided to take advantage of the skills he possessed, Greg helped add a whole new dimension to NFL quarterbacking.

In 1967, the great veteran, Fran Tarkenton, took time out to make a prophecy:

"I think the quarterback of tomorrow is going to be

better than we are today. He will be able to do a zillion things, including scrambling. He's going to have the ability to throw from the roll, the moving pocket, the dropback pocket, the bootleg, and the busted play. The quarterbacks coming out of the colleges nowadays are better athletes than ever before; they can do everything."

A year later Greg Landry arrived on the scene. He was bigger than most quarterbacks, standing 6-4 and weighing upwards of 215 pounds. When he ran, it wasn't just a scramble to escape a sacking. It was power running, fullback style, and he gained big yards by taking off.

That was the new dimension Greg brought to the NFL. When Tarkenton arrived on the scene in 1961 he introduced the new scrambling style to the league. But his scrambling was essentially used to give himself more time. Playing on an expansion team with an expansionist line in front of him, Fran was often chased from the pocket. Sometimes his scrambling gave him the time to find a secondary receiver, sometimes it enabled him to run for a good gain on his own.

Yet Fran Tarkenton wasn't a runner. He went out of bounds when he was cornered, or he'd fall down in the fetal position to avoid taking a hard hit.

With Greg Landry, it was different. From the time he called a quarterback sneak and ran up the middle for 76 yards during his third season, the Lions realized they had something special. So Greg became the first quarterback in more than twenty years to have running plays specifically designed in the team offense for him.

"Landry gives their offense a new dimension," said a rival defensive coach, Neil Armstrong of the Vikings. "When we get ready for the Lions we have to look upon Landry as a third running back as well as a passer. He was always capable of running, not scrambling, out of the pocket if his pass receivers were covered. He still does. But now they've put in a double option for him.

"He runs along the line and can either keep the ball or pitch it back to his halfback if the defense comes up too fast. It's running by design, not forced running, and that makes it much harder to stop."

Former Lion offensive coach Bill McPeak said the option was put in to take advantage of Greg's natural instincts and energies. "It also increased the likelihood that Greg would be hit by a 190-pound defensive back instead of a 250-pound lineman who might destroy him," McPeak said.

As for Greg himself, he's perfectly contented with the way things turned out as far as his running is concerned.

"I like to think of myself as a conventional dropback passer who can run," Greg said. "I'm not really a scrambler. I gain most of my yards on the option play, not by scrambling out of the pocket. I enjoy running, but not just for the sake of it. I realize that the injury factor increases when I run, but the option series is unique and puts the defense in a bind.

"The way we run the series there's not much chance for me to get a real shot. Most of the time our fullback is in front of me and he'll pick up the first guy trying to clobber me. Then I can either pitch the ball off or sneak through that first wave, cutting down the chances of me getting tackled that hard."

So the unique talents of Greg Landry enabled him to win the top job with the Lions, beating out a good dropback passer, Bill Munson, along the way. And Landry has been followed into the league by the likes of Roger Staubach, Terry Bradshaw, Archie Manning, Jim Plunkett, and Bobby Douglass, all of whom can handle themselves when they have to run the football. Douglass, in fact, ran for 968 yards a couple of years ago, besting the quarterback rushing record that Greg set in 1971. So it seems that Fran Tarkenton was right. The modern quarterback is a new breed of cat.

The first of the breed, Greg Landry, was born on December 18, 1946, in the town of Nashua, New Hampshire. It was a small, close-knit community where Mr. and Mrs. Alvin Landry lived near other members of their family and had many good friends. So young Greg grew up in a pleasant, small-town atmosphere and had a good childhood.

Greg was a youngster who took to sports early.

"As soon as I was old enough I'd be begging my dad to come out and play something with me. It might be baseball, basketball, or football. I loved them all. We'd either shoot baskets, throw a football around, or play pitch and catch. Like most kids I played whatever was in season.

"When I got a little older I started playing with the other kids in the neighborhood and we played all we could. At 12 I was real tall and real skinny, but I started playing Pop Warner football and was a quarter-

back for the first time. When I got to Nashua High
School I split between quarterback and defensive
back. I really liked playing defensive back because I
liked the hitting."

It was at Nashua High that Greg met coach Buzz
Harvey and his football development really took off.
It all began in the fall of 1961 when Greg played on
the varsity for the first time. Coach Harvey liked him
immediately, and also saw the great potential in the
gangly youngster.

"Greg was easy to coach from the first day he came
here," Harvey recalls. "He always gave 100 per cent,
listened well, and was a leader. The other boys
looked up to him."

Another old family friend, Joe Whelton, who is
Greg's lawyer today, remembers those early days at
Nashua.

"Greg was still pretty skinny when he started
playing high school ball," says Whelton. "He knew he
had to build himself up and he worked diligently to
do it. Every day I can remember him exercising with
weights and it showed. But Greg's always been like
that. He's mature enough to realize what he has to do
and then he goes ahead and does it."

Coach Harvey had been an All-American at Holy
Cross and was a shrewd judge of talent. From the
first time he met Greg he worked with the youngster.
Greg saw a lot of action as a sophomore, though the
coach didn't play him full time, not wanting to put
too much pressure on him too soon. But as a junior,
Greg began to blossom. He was getting bigger and
stronger, and putting together his natural physical
skills.

One day Coach Harvey asked Greg and a couple of other ballplayers if they wanted to go down to Holy Cross and watch his alma mater play Penn State. The boys went willingly. The Penn State quarterback that year was a guy named Pete Liske, and he was a good one. Liske ran from an offense that featured a triple option, a play controlled by the quarterback and enabling him to run, pitch out, or pass. Liske ran it well and drove the Holy Cross defense crazy all afternoon. Both Greg and Coach Harvey watched with interest.

When the coach told Greg the next week that he was thinking of trying a similar triple option, Greg licked his chops. Within a week it was part of the Nashua offense and Landry ran it perfectly. He could either give the ball to a plunging fullback, pitch it to his halfback, or keep it himself with an additional option to run or pass. He didn't make it a secret which he preferred.

"I kept it whenever I could," he said. "I loved to run the football."

Greg had a great junior year, leading Nashua to a winning season. He was well on his way to setting a host of school records, and that summer he worked even harder, hoping to help his club and his coach to another outstanding season.

When he returned in the fall of 1963 he was almost 6-3 and close to 200 pounds. He was also extremely fast, running the 40-yard dash in 4.7 seconds. And he was getting stronger all the time. Coach Harvey knew he had a great one in Greg.

"This boy has the will to win," the coach said before the season even started. "And he possesses the two most precious attributes of a great football player—

desire and determination. With these two qualities and his physical attributes, I see a tremendous future for him anywhere he goes."

But in the big game that year Nashua had to face Everett High. Everett had won the Massachusetts Class A state title two years in a row and was now gunning for a third. Nashua had lost a couple of close games and didn't figure in the title picture, but a victory over heavily-favored Everett would be a prize to remember, especially since Everett had taken 23 games in a row.

There was a light practice the day before the game, and when it was over Coach Harvey asked some of his individual players how they thought it would go the next day. Most of them voiced a very cautious optimism, fully aware of the devastating reputation of their opponent. But when the coach got to Greg Landry, he received an answer right out of the pages of *Frank Merriwell*.

"Don't worry, coach. We'll win it tomorrow!"

Coach Harvey remembers the incident well.

"I knew with Greg that it was an act of sincere confidence," he said. "It was also his way of trying to erase the concerned look I had on my face. I really was worried that my kids were going to be run off the field."

"Well, it didn't happen that way. Greg Landry had perhaps the greatest day of his high school career. He controlled the game, calling the triple option time and again, and often running himself. He was the star of the show, gaining big yardage on the ground and clicking on some key pass plays. Everett couldn't stop him. When the game ended, Nashua had a 20-6 upset victory.

After the game, the modest Landry refused to take credit for engineering the win. He cited his teammates and the overall team effort, not the least of which was the coaching job done by Buzz Harvey.

"That was typical Greg," said Harvey. "He was always modest, always giving the other guys credit. I guess that's why they liked and respected him so much. He's quite a guy."

From the Everett game to the end of the season the college scouts and recruiters swarmed around Greg. It didn't seem likely that Greg would stay in the area, not when the likes of Michigan State, Notre Dame, and Penn State were seriously pursuing him, with week-end trips to the campuses and personal visits with the coaches. The opportunity to play so-called big-time ball would surely be too much for any youngster to pass up.

But while many thought Greg would be trying to decide between the hotshot schools, the University of Massachusetts was entering the picture. It was a relatively small school which competed in the Yankee Conference against other local entries.

Ted Schmidt, the recruiter at U. Mass., had a low-key approach to his job. He didn't make a sales pitch, promising this and that. He simply told Greg what he thought the University could offer in the way of both athletic and educational programs. He also said that the school was more interested in Greg as a defensive back than as a quarterback.

Yet Greg surprised everyone by announcing he

would attend U. Mass. Years later, he talked about the biggest reason for his unexpected choice.

"Pro football was beyond my wildest dreams way back then," he confessed. "I wanted to be a coach; I was pretty sure of that. So I figured I ought to go to a New England school, a place where I could make a name for myself in the area. That would make it easier for me to get a coaching job near there."

Though Greg had been drafted as a defensive back, it didn't take U. Mass. coach Vic Fusia long to spot where his real talents lay. As his sophomore year began, Greg was the team's starting quarterback. He had a good supporting cast that year. His fullback was Phil Vandersea, who later had a shot as a linebacker at Green Bay, and the tight end was big Milt Morin, later a star for the Cleveland Browns. These two, combined with Landry, gave U. Mass. a tough offense right off the bat.

Once again Greg's roll-out talents were used well. If he didn't give the ball to Vandersea, he'd start moving with the option of throwing to Morin or another receiver, or keeping the ball himself. Naturally, he favored keeping it.

"Sure, I loved to run," Greg admits. "And when Vandersea and Morin graduated after the '65 season I carried more than ever since we couldn't replace those two guys."

As a sophomore, Greg was a poised performer, big and strong, and he could beat you in many ways. His very first varsity game against Maine saw him connect 12 of 21 passes for 190 yards. He also carried 22 times and gained 77 yards from scrimmage, though losses trying to pass brought his net down to 37 yards.

A week later he showed his speed by bolting 56 yards for a touchdown. Against Vermont several weeks after that he had a banner day passing, hitting on 20 of 25 tosses for 300 yards and three touchdowns. That's big league passing anywhere.

But Greg saved his best performance for last, the season finale against New Hampshire. In that game he was the whole show. He passed for 192 yards, a 12-for-22 day including a touchdown. That was just act one. As a runner he was even more devastating, galloping for 204 big yards on just 13 carries, including TD runs of 48 and 20 yards. He was virtually unstoppable, as U. Mass. closed with a 7-2 record and a 4-1 mark in Yankee Conference play, good for second place.

"Greg is a real student of the game," said Coach Fusia. "He studies constantly, watching movies of our opponents and looking for defensive flaws. And if he sees a flaw, he'll exploit it. There's nothing he likes better than picking a defense apart.

"He's also got a lightning-quick mind on the field. When he's out there he's actually reading the defense and not many college quarterbacks do that well. But I've seen him spot something, make a split-second decision at the line, and invariably, his new play works."

Greg had an unbelievable year in 1965. He completed 96 of 154 passes for 1,423 yards and eight touchdowns. His completion percentage was high at .623. As a rusher he carried 134 times for a net of 614 yards. He actually gained 853 yards on those carries, but lost 239 while attempting to pass. He scored another nine touchdowns on the ground and produced a total offense mark of 2,037.

He set several school and conference records that very first year. His total offense of 1,293 yards in five Y.C. games was a new mark, as was his net rushing yardage of 614.

The next two years were much harder for Greg in that he didn't have the supporting cast around him and had to take on a greater share of the offensive load. Yet he still led his team to two straight Yankee Conference titles, winning all 10 conference games in which he played. Overall, the club was 6-3 in '66 and 7-2 in 1967, so Greg stayed a big winner throughout.

His stats fell off somewhat in '66, though he rebounded well during his senior year. That season he threw for 991 yards and six TD's, as well as gaining a net of 728 on 177 rushes. He had another banner running day against Connecticut that year, gaining 200 yards on 21 carries, scoring on runs of 34, 1, and 73 yards, and averaging almost 10 yards a tote.

Against Rhode Island his club was behind with just minutes remaining. The ball was at the Rhode Island 34 when Greg called for a pitchout to his halfback. But the back went the wrong way and when Greg whirled to hand off the ball, no one was there.

But he didn't panic. He just tucked the ball under his arm, cut off tackle, straight-armed a linebacker, faked the safety, and sprinted 34 yards to the end zone with the winning score.

There were some other big games. Holy Cross was beating U. Mass. by a 21-14 count with time running out. Greg's friend Joe Whelton, remembers that one well.

"It looked all over," Whelton says. "We had the ball on our own 10 and there was something like a minute left. But Greg was calm. He simply started to throw. He rifled home three strikes in a row—boom, boom, boom. Just like that and we had a touchdown. That made it 21-20. We decided to go for two points and the win. Greg rifled another strike to a guy open in the end zone ... but he dropped it and we lost. Still, I couldn't believe how great Greg had been in that last minute."

In Greg's U. Mass. career, he completed 242 of 445 passes for 3,131 yards, 16 touchdowns, and a .544 percentage. He rushed 485 times for a net of 1,632 yards and another 22 scores. He set 13 school records, most of them for rushing, passing, and total offense. It was an outstanding college scorecard, and it didn't go unnoticed.

The fact that both of Greg's teammates his sophomore year, Vandersea and Morin, had made NFL clubs focused a little more attention on U. Mass. Scouts were sniffing around to see what the Landry kid was all about.

One of the scouts was Bobby Layne, the former great quarterback of the Detroit Lions and Pittsburgh Steelers. Layne came up to watch the final game of the 1967 season against a rough-tough Boston College team. U. Mass. didn't win that game. In fact, they took a terrible physical beating from the much bigger B.C. gridders. Statistically Greg didn't have a banner day, but he stood up so well against a hard-charging line and vicious gang-tackling that he made as good an impression as if he had passed for five TD's against lesser opposition.

There were many local post-season honors, including the Bulger Lowe Award, given annually by the

Gridiron Club of Boston to the outstanding New England collegiate football player, and that didn't include just Yankee Conference Schools. Greg was the winner hands down.

Greg still wasn't sure about a pro football career. While he was confident going up against Yankee Conference opposition, he had no idea what it was like playing against major schools and All-America players. Sure, he was an All-America, but only on the college division team, so when an invitation came to play in the annual North-South all-star game, Greg accepted quickly.

"I figured I might as well find out just what I could do against the big boys," he said.

What he did was throw two touchdowns passes for the North squad against a star-studded South club. He also called a cool, intelligent game and the North won it, 14-0. Suddenly, Greg Landry had all kinds of new-found confidence.

"It was my first time against guys from all the top-rated football schools and you can't imagine what those two TD passes did for me. It made me begin to believe that I was as good as any other quarterback around, no matter what school he played for."

So for the first time, Greg began concentrating on the pro draft, which was only weeks away. A few years before, the pros had been beyond his wildest dreams. Now they weren't. He began thinking about playing professional football, wondering what it would be like to quarterback a pro team. If he had only known what was taking place in Detroit about that time, he really would have been excited.

The Lions were one of the original NFL teams

with a long tradition. They had had their good years, winning several NFL titles along the way. Scout Bobby Layne himself may have been the best quarterback they ever had, and since Bobby's departure as an active player, the team had been searching for a successor.

During 1967 the job had been shared by veteran Milt Plum and young Carl Sweetan. Neither showed enough for club officials to plan a future with him. So the search was on. And after scanning the nation's prospects, general manager Russ Thomas and club owner Bill Ford singled out Greg Landry as the player they most wanted. In doing so they passed up Gary Beban of UCLA, the quarterback who had just been awarded the Heisman Trophy, emblematic of the nation's best collegiate player.

One man disagreed with Thomas and Ford. He was Joe Schmidt. And since he happened to be the head coach he had to be listened to. Schmidt felt the Lions had a good array of talent and wanted to trade for an experienced quarterback who could blend right in with the other veterans. The argument became so heated that Schmidt actually shouted, "I quit," and left the room.

But Schmidt thought things over, returned, and said, "OK, you're probably right that Landry will be the best bet in the long run. He's got all the physical tools. But it's going to take him a good three years. He won't be a magic man and come right out of college to lead us to the promised land. I'll go along with the draft if you'll let me keep shopping around for a veteran."

Thomas and Ford agreed, and in January they tabbed Greg Landry as their number one pick.

"To tell you the truth," said Russ Thomas, "we've been interested in Greg for a long time and we were really surprised that some team above us didn't pick him. All our reports on him have been excellent."

There was criticism from the fans. How could the club pass up a Heisman Trophy winner like Beban for a kid who had played against Class C opposition?

"We picked the physical man and not his opposition," said Thomas. "We know that Greg is almost 6-4 and well over 200 pounds. Plus he's fast, very durable, loves the game, has a strong arm and can throw long or short. He's a fine boy and very intelligent on the ball field. We picked him strictly on those qualifications."

Thomas went on to point out how players like John Unitas and Bart Starr had been virtual unknowns and had been drafted on very low rounds.

"You never know about quarterbacks," he said. "The good ones can come from anywhere."

As for Greg, he was simply ecstatic. He said he was only interested in playing football and that his old friend, Joe Whelton, would handle the financial end of it.

There was some hassling over the contract and some rumors that the Lions were having second thoughts about choosing Greg. But both crises were averted. Greg signed and the team officials unanimously welcomed him to the organization. However, Schmidt also got his way. Before the season started the Lions acquired veteran Bill Munson from the Los

Angeles Rams. He was immediately listed as the starting quarterback with Greg as the backup.

In June, Greg was down in Atlanta to quarterback the East squad in the annual Coaches All-America game. There was some added pressure on him. He knew that everyone watching was well aware that he went to the University of Massachusetts. Now he was playing with and against the so-called best. In fact, Gary Beban was slated to go against Greg for the West team.

"No one has come up to me and said it," Greg told a reporter, "but I can feel that they're all thinking it. They're thinking, 'What the heck is a kid from a small New England school doing here? Detroit must have made a mistake.' 'How does it feel to play big-time football?' And they're going to keep thinking this until I prove myself."

Greg had some added pressure. Though never injured in a college game, he had hurt his ankle helping some underclassmen at U. Mass. spring practice.

"It was in a cast for three weeks and it's still swollen," he said. "I've got to tape it heavily but it's not really hindering me now. I'm not going to use it as an excuse.

"As for Beban, sure, I've had a lot of questions about going against him. But in a game like this, with all the great players, no one individual is going to make that much difference. Gary is a great quarterback. But I'm not really concerned about playing opposite him because I'll have some great players out in front of me helping make it a team effort."

Greg looked sharp in practice, connecting with his receivers and making as much of a "big-time" impression as anyone else. John Pont of Indiana, the coach of the East team, had only good things to say about his New England quarterback.

"Greg has that good quick release of the football," said Pont, "and that's something you always wonder about in an untried quarterback.. He's had an ankle injury and he's still looked good. I know he's aware that he's the only player from New England in camp here and he wants to have a good game. Don't sell him short."

The game turned into a passing war. Gary Beban had a great day. He completed 15 of 20 for 222 yards, including a clutch, 44-yard touchdown toss in the closing minutes which won the ballgame. As for Greg, though on the losing end, he pretty much proved what he wanted. He had a fine game, connecting on 16 of 24 passes for 160 yards.

Beban got most of the press notices, but a lot of pro coaches and scouts were more impressed by Landry, the way he threw, his size, his poise. They still rated him a better prospect than the smaller Beban.

A month later the two quarterbacks were teammates, this time at the College All-Star camp preparing to meet the world champion Green Bay Packers. Again the reporters gathered around asking questions and expecting Greg to have all the answers.

"Beban had a great day at the Coaches' game," Greg said. "My team lost, but I was satisfied that I did a good job. Now Gary and I are working together and there's no rivalry between us. We try to help each other every way we can.

"I've been reading the stuff about Gary being too short, but he's got a strong arm. He rolled out a lot in college but I think he can correct this. I have things to correct, too. I've got to be able to read defenses quickly, drop back fast, spot the coverage, and look for a certain open man and hit him.

"Coach Van Brocklin says Gary and I will split the QB work and we're both looking forward to the game. But I feel the way a lot of guys do, that we're losing time in our own camps and would probably be better off learning our own systems."

That's a prevalent attitude almost every year in the All-Star camp. But the rookies can learn there and this crop was no different. They learned how tough the Green Bay Packers were. The Pack won easily, though Greg played well, this time better than Beban according to most observers. It was hard passing to unfamiliar receivers, especially against the big Packer rush. But he again showed poise, toughness, and his fine running ability, which never left him.

After the game he got to the Lions' camp as quickly as he could. There he soon found out that Bill Munson was a good professional quarterback. He had come up with the Rams in 1964, playing very well when Roman Gabriel was injured. Munson won the starting job the next year, only to lose it back to Gabriel. He hadn't played much in '66 and '67 and was anxious to be a number one man again.

Munson was a much more disciplined quarterback than Greg. He was strictly a dropback passer, and a good one, cool and accurate. Though not quite as big as Greg, Munson had good size at 6-2 and 205 pounds. He'd be tough to dislodge, and Greg knew it.

"I know I'm not going to step in and be a star overnight," he said. "It's a long learning process, a gradual thing. Many people say it takes four or five years, but I hope it's a lot quicker than that.

"Bill has four years' experience behind him and he has to be number one. I might not be able to challenge him this year, but maybe some time next year I'll start to come on. If not, then the year after that. Just about every number one in this league has been a number two at one time or another. But when you're number two you tend to study more, sit and learn, and the more you want to play. Any quarterback who sits on the bench and is satisfied ought to quit football."

Greg surely wasn't in the big time for laughs. Once he realized he could play pro ball his old fire and competitiveness returned. He wanted to be a starter now, a leader and a winning quarterback. He had signed a three-year, $125,000 package with the Lions and he wanted to earn it.

"When you're not playing and you pick up your paycheck every Monday," he said, "you begin to feel as if you're not earning it. Sometimes you don't even feel like part of the team."

Though Munson was a veteran, he was still new to the Lions and had to learn their system. And since he hadn't seen much action during the two preceding seasons, the coaching staff figured he needed all the work he could get. He saw the brunt of the action in the exhibition season. In fact, Greg got into just portions of two games. In two others he didn't play at all. Now there was one exhibition left with the New York Jets, then the regular season would begin.

Greg was in an awkward position. He liked Munson and the older quarterback was helping him greatly. He also knew that Munson needed work. Yet he needed it, too, and both of them couldn't play at one time.

"Bill has a great football mind," Greg said. "He's really been helping me with reading defenses and other phases of quarterbacking. I know he needs the work if he's going to do the job. I'm sure we can win with him this year.

"As for myself, I want to play as much as possible. It's the only way you can learn. I think I came here knowing more than other rookie quarterbacks, enough to put me at least a full season ahead in development. Credit for this goes to my college coach, Vic Fusia.

"Vic spent a lot of time with me. He would go over the weaknesses of an opponent and their defenses every Monday, even before we discussed our offense. He showed me what to look for and how to exploit a weakness. He taught me the value of using a balanced attack. I'd say we passed about 40 per cent of the time at U. Mass., and that's just about our ratio here.

"But there are big differences, don't get me wrong. In college you worry about one defense. That's it. Here you've got about five or six coming at you each game, and all of them are cleverly disguised. So you've got to wait that split second before dropping back and try to read the key to each defense. It takes experience to do that and you've got to play to get the experience."

Greg wasn't complaining, just stating his position, the way it was at that time in 1968. Munson was at the helm again when Detroit went up against the Jets in the final pre-season contest.

Both clubs had first stringers in there, getting tuned up for their openers, and they were hitting. Late in the second quarter Munson dropped back to pass, couldn't find a receiver, and was buried by three Jets. When he got up he was holding his side and he came to the sideline. Suddenly, Greg Landry was in the game.

Munson had bruised ribs and strained stomach muscles, so Greg would have to go the rest of the way. He played well, but fumbles and penalties frittered away scoring opportunities. The Jets won, 9-6.

Greg hated to see Munson hurt, though he enjoyed the playing time, especially against a good defensive team like the Jets. After the game, Greg learned that Munson might not be ready for the opener against Dallas the following week. On Wednesday, Coach Schmidt told Greg he'd be the starting quarterback. News like that might have caused panic in some youngsters, but not Landry. He was confident.

"I know I can go out there and move the team," he said. "I'm not about to disgrace myself and I won't disgrace the Lions. Maybe I've only played in three games, but I've been with the club for five and I've gained a lot of confidence. A quarterback has got to have confidence if he expects to do the job."

So the stage was set. The Lions had compiled a 5-7-2 record in '67 and were looking for a solid rebuilding year. And they'd get an immediate test, since Dallas had one of the most powerful clubs in the entire league.

The first time the Lions had the ball, Greg came out onto the field. It was a long way from Nashua High and U. Mass. Now he was facing the famed

"Doomsday Defense," 11 men who had been known to make all-pro quarterbacks eat humble pie. Greg figured, what the heck, he might as well come out winging.

Perhaps it was his tactics that threw the Cowboys. They hadn't expected a raw rookie to come out throwing, but Greg did. The first time he dropped back and threw, he connected with a receiver. Then he did it again. Bullseye. The third time the result was the same. So were the fourth and fifth. And the sixth was grabbed in the end zone for a touchdown.

Greg Landry had completed his first six passes as a pro, the last being a TD toss, and the Lions took a 7-0 lead. It was right out of fairyland.

"I didn't know a thing about defenses when you came down to it," he said later. "I just stepped into the pocket and threw to the right color jersey. Somehow it worked and I left the field thinking that pro ball was a lot easier than everyone said."

But fairyland isn't the real world, as Greg learned a few minutes later. He was back out there and thinking in terms of another touchdown. He saw his fine tight end, Charlie Sanders, wide open with linebacker Chuck Howley turned the wrong way. He cranked and threw. But Greg had never seen a linebacker as fast as Chuck Howley. He recovered and intercepted the ball before it reached Sanders.

"How the heck did he do that?" Greg muttered as he left the field.

Greg was to learn a lot about linebackers that afternoon. Three more times the Cowboys backers intercepted his passes. Within minutes the game had turned around. Though Greg finally threw for another TD late in the game, Dallas won in a rout, 59-13.

Despite the four intercepts and having to play catch-up ball most of the game, Greg did very well. He connected on 15 of 31 passes for 231 yards and two scores. Those are major league stats, though the big loss didn't say much for the Detroit defense.

A week later Munson was back, and Greg resumed his learning process on the sideline. He saw very little action the rest of the year, though the team wasn't going anywhere. There were still many holes to be filled.

In November, he told reporters, "The fog is beginning to lift. I'm seeing more things, understanding more, and learning."

Then he got another start, in game 12, on a rain-soaked field against the winless Philadelphia Eagles. Munson had a slight injury and Coach Schmidt didn't want to risk him on the slippery field. That day the Eagles' losing streak stopped. They won, 12-0, as Greg completed just seven of 15 for only 66 yards. "It was another humbling experience," he said.

The season ended with the Lions at 4-8-2 and in last place in the Central Division. In addition to the two starts, Greg saw very limited action in three other games. Overall, he completed 23 of 48 for 338 yards and two scores. He had seven passes intercepted. He ran the ball just seven times and gained 39 yards.

Munson was again number one for the Lions when the 1969 season got underway. Greg was resigned to another year of backup duty, but he was working as hard as ever, trying to learn all he could as fast as he could. He served notice that he wasn't content with being number two and that he'd be challenging Munson soon. And it couldn't come quickly enough to suit him.

With Munson again playing well, the Lions won two of their first three, then came up against the Packers. Late in the game Bill dropped back to pass. He threw the ball and his arm followed through. At that second, linebacker Dave Robinson came charging at him and Munson's hand slammed hard into Robinson's helmet. The hand was hurt, badly. Greg came in and finished the game, a 28-17 loss that brought the team back to 2-2. After the game, word came through that Munson had a fractured bone in his throwing hand. He'd be out five or six weeks. Suddenly, Greg was in. As Coach Schmidt said:

"Well, we'll get Mr. Landry up and ready to play and we'll go on from there."

Greg was happy to get a shot, but not happy about the way it happened.

"I'm sorry that I'm breaking in this way, at Bill's expense," he said. "I hate to see any teammate get hurt. But I've got a lot of confidence and I feel everyone will pull together behind me. I think they have confidence in me, too. No one will be biting their fingernails."

The Lions were home facing the Bears in Greg's first start. The Chicagoans were a tough bunch and Greg didn't want to take any chances. He called a conservative, ball-control game, passing only when he had to and showing signs of his great running ability from college days. The Lions won, 13-7, and Greg had his first victory as a pro.

But once again there was a rude awakening. The

Lions traveled up to Minnesota to meet the division-leading Vikings, and they got pushed all over the field. The great Vike front four of Carl Eller, Alan Page, Gary Larsen, and Jim Marshall punished Greg unmercifully, pursuing him all over the field and treating him the way vets usually treat youngsters, trying to show him what the NFL is all about and giving him a lesson to remember in the future. They didn't intimidate Greg, but they did hurt him.

"It was my ankle," Greg said. "I got it in the third quarter on a sprint out. It caved in just before we scored."

Greg had to leave the game, and third-string QB Greg Barton finished up. The Vikings won it, 24-10, and Landry left town on crutches. Suddenly he faced the prospect of giving up the job the same way Munson had relinquished it.

"I thought about that as soon as I got hurt. At first I refused to come out of the game," Greg said. "I just don't leave ballgames, I told them. You'll have to carry me out to get me out. And they did. They had to; the ankle was bad."

The next day the ankle was put in a cast to immobilize it. The diagnosis was a bad sprain, with the healing time unpredictable. By Thursday Greg had resumed practice, but with a noticeable limp. The game plan for Sunday's action at San Francisco listed Barton as the starting quarterback.

Greg was still hobbling on Saturday. But all he could think of was the game and convincing Schmidt that he could get ready. When the teams went out for warmup at Kezar Stadium on Sunday, Greg concentrated on trying not to limp. Schmidt saw him, knew how badly he wanted to play, and decided to take a chance.

"I didn't think he could get back up on it," Schmidt said. "This morning was the first time he could even turn on it."

So Greg was in there when the game started. The 49ers knew he was hurt and put on the big rush. They trapped him time and again, burying him with gang-tackling and trying to put him out of the game.

But Greg hung in there. He didn't have his usual running ability and was hard pressed to escape the rush. Yet in the fourth period with the outcome still very much in doubt, Greg dropped back and arched a pass in the direction of Charlie Sanders.

"When I threw the pass I got knocked down," Greg remembers. "Then I got up and listened for the crowd reaction. I heard cheers. I thought it was an interception. Then I saw the San Francisco guy with his back to me and he didn't have the ball. Charlie had it and was running into the end zone!"

The Lions had won it, 26-14. Greg was trapped so many times that he didn't have a very big offensive yield statistically, but he had won the game.

"That game showed me what kind of guts Greg Landry had," said Coach Schmidt. "He shouldn't have played the game at all, but he did. The ankle was swollen so badly that he couldn't run. But somehow he managed. He was in a great deal of pain the whole way. What it amounted to was that he sacrificed for the good of the team."

Greg had to prop his leg up to reduce the terrible pain as the club left San Francisco by airplane. Still, he talked to a reporter about leading the team.

"I can't worry about statistics," he said. "The important thing is leading the team. Look at Joe Kapp. He may be two for 20, but both those will be touchdowns and his team wins. That's the important thing, leading the ballclub and winning."

After the Frisco game both Greg and the Lions got hot, rolling over Atlanta, St. Louis, and Green Bay. The team was 7-3 and trailing 9-1 Minnesota in the divisional race. And it was showdown time. There was also another showdown before the two teams met. Munson had recovered from his hand injury and was now activated. Schmidt had to decide which QB to start.

"I decided to go with Landry," he explained. "The club knows he can do the job and has confidence in him. I don't want to mess with that feeling at all."

The big game was played on Thanksgiving Day before a national television audience. It was a game Greg would like to forget. The Lions' offensive wall couldn't stop the powerful Viking defense, and they were all over Greg like a swarm of bees. He couldn't generate any kind of offense. In the fourth quarter defensive end Carl Eller came pouncing in on Greg's shoulder. The strain on his throwing arm put him out again. Munson finished the 27-0 loss, then finished out the year. The Lions were 9-4-1, their best record in years, and finished second in the division.

Greg was a 50-per cent passer in '69, completing 80 of 160 in 10 games. His throws gained 853 yards and were good for four touchdowns. He still had 10 intercepts, but began showing some of his great running ability, gaining 243 yards on just 33 carries for a 7.4 average. Yet he knew the starting job wasn't his. Now he felt he was ready, but he'd have to compete with Munson once again in 1970. And this time the Lions were talking playoffs.

When training camp started Coach Schmidt said the QB job was up for grabs. Camp and the exhibitions would decide who started, and the coach said he hoped he could settle on one man and stay with him for the whole year. It was hard to say just who the coach would choose. Both quarterbacks had proved they could win. But that's where the similarity ended. Their styles were as different as night and day.

"Bill is the prototype of the dropback passer," Greg said, "whereas I typify the young quarterbacks coming into the league today. If you want a picture passer you don't want Greg Landry. But I'm not here to be a picture passer, I'm here to complete them when I have to and win."

Many observers thought Schmidt would go with Landry. He was younger and could seemingly do more things. But when the final exhibition game rolled around Munson was the starter, and when it ended, Schmidt said that Munson would open the regular season.

Greg was confused and frustrated. He wasn't sure why the coach had made that pick, but figured it was still the experience factor. And the next week he watched Munson perform brilliantly against the Green Bay Packers, opening up a huge lead before Greg got in late in the game.

The Lions had the ball on their own 13, a third-and-two situation. Greg wanted to run out the clock and elected to give the ball to his fullback. But he changed the play at the line, calling a quarterback sneak. He took the ball and charged straight ahead. He felt arms grabbing at him, but pulled free, then looked up and faked a linebacker. Suddenly he was in the clear—and he bolted 76 yards before being dragged down from behind. It was one of the longest quarterback sneaks of all time. P.S.: Detroit won, 40-0.

Despite Greg's electrifying run, Munson was the quarterback again the following week. This time he whipped Cincinnati, 38-3, then came back to lead the team over Chicago, 28-14. The Lions were 3-0 and everyone was getting excited. Greg was happy for the team, but with Munson playing so well, he saw his own prospects slipping away.

Then the next week the club and Munson suddenly did a turnabout, losing to Washington, 31-10. Wins over Cleveland and Chicago followed, then a loss to Minnesota, putting the club at 5-2. The next week Munson had his poorest day, throwing three intercepts against New Orleans. The Saints had a 16-10 lead late in the final session. That's when Schmidt finally called on Landry.

Greg immediately drove the team downfield for a score, making it 17-16. There were seconds left and he should have the win. But fate intervened. Tom Dempsey booted a record 63-yard field goal and the Saints pulled it out, 19-17. But the game was a turning point. It handed the top job back to Greg.

"I came to camp this year with the idea of being number one," Greg told a reporter. "Then the coach opened with Bill. I've been waiting for my chance now and I've got to make good. If I don't do the job

Coach will go back to Bill and I can't blame him. He's got to go with the guy who'll get him the wins."

So Greg took that attitude into his first start against Minnesota. He played very well, getting the Lions into a 10-point lead. Only this time the defense fell apart and the Vikes came back to win it, 24-20. Now the club was at 5-4 and suddenly the whole prospect of making the playoffs looked bleak. But Greg Landry wasn't through.

If the Lions lost another one it could mean disaster, and the tough San Francisco 49ers were next. But the defense tightened and Greg did the rest. He controlled the football and threw three scoring passes to lead his club to a 28-7 victory.

After the game, Coach Schmidt said: "You played great, Greg, but try not to run so much."

The next week the Oakland Raiders struck early and took a 14-0 lead on the Lions. Greg didn't panic as an inexperienced quarterback might. He coolly led his team back, throwing for three more scores and running for another 77 yards as the Lions rallied for a 28-14 win.

"I'm trying to get away from running," Greg said after the game. "But when I'm forced into it I won't avoid it. I'm confident in my running and feel it's a positive weapon."

Finally, Joe Schmidt had to agree. "Greg's a great runner. I try not to worry about him. He's big enough so that if he gets by the linemen and linebackers he shouldn't get hurt. If he only runs when he has to he gives us a good play. This is what we've been working on and this is where Greg has improved."

It was uphill the rest of the way. Greg led the

Lions to three more wins, over St. Louis, Los Angeles, and Green Bay. The team finished the season with a 10-4 mark and entered the playoffs as a wild card entry from the NFC West.

Greg's stats showed his marked improvement. He threw the ball 136 times, 24 fewer passes than in '69. Yet he completed three more, 83, for a 61 per cent figure. His yardage was up to 1,072 and he tossed nine TD's and only five intercepts. As a runner he carried 35 times for 350 yards, and that's an average of 10 big yards per carry. In addition, he led his club into the playoffs for the first time in years and no other Lion quarterback since Bobby Layne had been able to do that.

In the playoff game, the club met the powerful Dallas Cowboys. The game quickly settled into a defensive battle. It was not a good day for Greg. Nothing he tried seemed to work. His fumble on one run led to a Dallas field goal. Later, he was trapped in the end zone for a safety. Schmidt even turned to Munson who almost pulled it out at the end. But an interception killed the final Detroit drive and Dallas won it by an unusual 5-0 score.

It was in the off-season that the fireworks started. Greg was finishing out his first three-year pact with the club and asked for a raise in his base salary from about $25,000 to $60,000. The Lions balked.

"I consider myself the number one quarterback now," Greg said. "Maybe Bill feels the same way. I do know that the Lions have two good quarterbacks and it's essentially up to the coach who plays. But I feel I'm worth a certain amount of money and I'd like to get it."

But the Lions wouldn't budge. Greg's old friend Joe Whelton was again doing the negotiating. When camp started Greg still hadn't signed and he announced he was playing out his option. That meant if he didn't sign by the end of the year he'd be a free agent and could sign with another team. It was a calculated gamble.

"Greg put himself under tremendous pressure," said Joe Whelton. "He was the quarterback, the team leader, and he had to work with players who had signed. He also had to work closely with coaches who wanted him to sign. Plus the other guys knew he was asking for more than they were getting. That situation usually creates tensions."

There was a chance that the Lions would just ignore Greg and turn to Munson. But the other quarterback was also playing out his option. So, since neither had signed, they were on an equal basis again and Greg was named the starter when the 1971 season began.

It was a strange year for the Lions. The team had other internal problems besides two unsigned quarterbacks.

Before the year started, veteran defensive tackle Alex Karras was cut. It came as a shock. He had been an all-pro for years, and most people figured that the cut involved more than just football ability. It hurt the team defense. Then, in the sixth game of the year, wide receiver Chuck Hughes collapsed on the field and died of a massive heart attack. The trauma of that experience took something out of the entire team. The club was 4-1 when Hughes died, 3-5-1 after. That made for a 7-6-1 year, a year that had held a world of promise three months before.

For Greg there were plenty of personal triumphs. He finally played an entire season and established himself as one of the great young quarterbacks in pro ball. In the fourth game against Green Bay he led his club to a 31-28 victory by connecting on four TD passes and throwing for 302 yards. He also made a believer out of Packer coach Dan Devine.

"I realize that Landry had a great day passing," said the Packer coach. "But I've always contended that a quarterback gets hurt passing, not running and it was Landry's running, not his passing, that really killed us. He used it to get out of our containment on third-down plays.

"He really proved what I've thought all along, that he's a good quarterback. He runs well and throws well. And he's really hard to stop."

Even late in the season, when the defense was falling apart and the club floundering, Greg was giving it his best. In a game with the Eagles the Lions were trailing, 16-13, with two minutes left. They had a third and goal at the Eagles' five-yard line. Greg called a pass, dropped back, and saw all his receivers covered.

Then he saw a hole and took off. He bulled past one defender, then was hit by linebacker Tim Rossovich at about the one. He continued to drive forward as Al Nelson and Ron Porter rushed up to help Rossovich. Greg wouldn't quit. He lowered his head and drove into the colliding mass of bodies. Somehow he flipped over them and landed in the end zone. It was an amazingly determined run.

But Greg didn't get up. He had a concussion, and had to be helped from the field.

"I knew I'd get hit," he said. "But if I was going to get creamed I wanted it to be in the end zone. I go out to win a football game and do what I have to. If it requires getting hit, I'll get hit."

Unfortunately, the defense wasn't tuned to Greg's heroics. They let the Eagles zip 79 yards in five plays and lost the game, 23-20, with Munson making a rare appearance for the final series. It had been a typical Landry day, 14 of 23 passes for 230 yards and seven rushes for 42 yards.

So the mediocre season ended. Greg was one of the few bright spots. He had an all-pro year, completing 136 of 261 passes for 2,237 yards and a 52.1 per cent average. He had thrown for 16 touchdowns as opposed to 13 intercepts. He also tuned up his running ability with a record 530 yards on 76 carries, for an average of seven yards a tote. He had a long gain of 52 yards and scored three times on the ground.

As the off-season began, Greg's salary squabble intensified. He had played through the option year, and if he didn't sign by the following spring he's be a free agent. There were all kinds of stories about secret, illegal negotiations with other teams, a big offer of $500,000 from Montreal of the Canadian League and continued threats by Greg that he would leave Detroit. He said he wanted to stay with the Lions, but his 1971 season proved he was worth more money.

"I looked at the situation and tried to ask for a fair figure," he said. "I feel I'm worth more than they've offered, in fact, I've even asked for less than my attorney wanted me to ask for."

A stellar performance in the Pro Bowl game that year solidified Greg's credentials. Against the best players in the AFC he completed six of 11 passes for 122 yards and ran for another 20. He was the best of the four quarterbacks who played in the game.

Finally, in the first week of May, Greg and the Lions came to terms. The team must have realized that he was a valuable piece of football property and they paid to keep him. The new pact was estimated to be in the $400,000 range covering the next three years. There was a huge bonus set at about $90,000, and the rest was salary. He had gambled and won.

In 1972, the Lion offense was tailored especially for Greg. The club installed pre-arranged option plays to take greater advantage of his running ability. He was established now, and happy.

On paper, the Lions seemed to have a powerful team. Offensively they had fine players, runners like Steve Owens, Mel Farr, and Altie Taylor, receivers such as Charlie Sanders, Larry Walton, Earl McCullouch, and Ron Jessie. Perhaps there were too many stars. They didn't always jell.

Defensively, the team had problems. They couldn't seem to rebuild. When Coach Schmidt was an all-pro linebacker and Karras an all-pro tackle, the Detroit defense was feared round the league. But now the young players weren't coming on fast enough, and the veterans were giving a spotty performance. Just when it seemed they were on the brink of moving, they'd lose a key game.

There was a loss to Minnesota, another one to Green Bay, then Dallas, then the Vikes again, all in key spots in the season. That left the club at 5-4 and struggling. Wins over New Orleans and the Jets put them back in the playoff picture, but then Green Bay did them in again, and a weak Buffalo team played them to a tie. A final win over the Rams meant nothing. The club was 8-5-2 and out of the playoffs. Green Bay won the division with the Lions second, but not good enough for a wild card berth.

Greg wasn't at all happy with his performance. He blamed injuries to his receivers and his own poor throwing at times. Someone pointed out that he had a personal hand in 22 touchdowns in the team's first 11 games, 13 by throwing, nine by running, but that didn't make it any easier to take. Missing the playoffs was the big thing.

Statistically Greg was 134 for 268, 50 per cent passing, good for 2,066 yards and 18 touchdowns. He also ran for another 524 yards and scored nine times on the ground. That isn't a bad season at all.

The Lions made a coaching change in 1973, replacing Joe Schmidt with Don McCafferty, who had coached Baltimore to a Super Bowl win a few seasons earlier. The new coach renewed the Landry-Munson rivalry, but opened the year with Greg. The old rap about him favoring the run over the pass was still around.

"I ran a lot out of necessity last season," Greg said. "I pride myself on my passing, I always have, but we didn't have that many good passing plays in the past. Coach McCafferty has given us a more liberal passing attack and I think we will be throwing more on so-called running downs than we have in the past."

But there were still defensive troubles and perhaps

morale problems. After six games, the club was 1-4-1 and already out of it. Greg was crushed.

"We have to win desperately now. Every game is important because the whole city is down on us and the only thing that will make up for it is winning. I think we still have a good football team, but not a great one. There are just too many new people on the roster and a new coaching staff to adjust to."

Two days later on October 26, Greg went into the Packer game. In the first quarter he was hit hard from the side while back to pass and injured his knee. He had the club in a 10-0 lead at the time. Munson finished up, holding on for the win.

Doctors suspected that Greg had cartilage damage, but did not recommend immediate surgery. About a week later they made the decision.

"The knee is swelling whenever he works on it," said Coach McCafferty. "That's a sign that something's wrong. They're going to operate."

So Greg had the first serious injury of his career. He had played in seven games and had completed 70 of 128 passes for 908 yards and three TD's. However, he was also intercepted 10 times, not a good ratio. He was still running a lot, with 267 yards on 42 tries. Munson would now finish the year.

It was pointed out that Greg had a 22-16-3 record as a starter. He was a winner. He always had been. But the Lions finished out the year on the losing side, and faced another rebuilding job. Munson played well in Greg's absence, completing over 51 per cent of his throws for more than 1,000 yards and tossing nine TD's. He's still a first-rank quarterback.

So in 1974 Greg Landry was at a crossroads. He

had to come back from the surgery. And he had to win back his job. He has shown all-pro ability, but has been criticised at times for his play selection and an inability to win the big one. But that criticism falls on the rest of the team as well.

Yet Greg knows he's the leader. When asked about not winning the big one he said:

"The quarterback is being paid the money so I guess he's the one who's blamed if things don't go right. I have to accept that. I don't necessarily believe it. I remember three years ago when we had to win five straight to make the playoffs and we did. Weren't those big games? I know we lost to Dallas that year but it wasn't choking, it was just making mistakes. There have been times I haven't played well, and times some other guys haven't played well.

"But the guy who usually gets blamed is the quarterback and he must live with it. Look at John Brodie. For 15 years people have called him a choke artist. Yet how many teams wouldn't trade for a guy like him if they had the chance."

So Greg's head is pretty straight. He knows all about big-time ball, and he always knew about it, even in his days at a so-called small-time college. He had what it takes then and he has it now. There have been ups and downs, triumphs and defeats. But he's shown the ability to rank up there with the best. And he's still got the time to do it. Greg Landry will be doing his thing for many years to come.

Roger Staubach

When the 1964 professional football draft rolled around, all the teams in both the National and American Leagues began looking over the crop of collegians available to them. General managers met with their coaching staffs, while scouts telephoned in reports from every corner of the land. The most common question asked about a player was: "Where can he fit into our immediate plans?"

Fortunately, Tex Schramm and the rest of his Dallas Cowboy organization had more foresight than that. Sure, they wanted to strengthen their team. The Cowboys had been formed in 1960 and had just completed a 4-10 season. They needed help.

And they drafted for it. Then came the 10th round. Schramm surprised everyone. He made his choice and it was announced at NFL headquarters.

"The Cowboys pick Roger Staubach, quarterback, Navy."

Roger Staubach? The Cowboys must be crazy! First of all, Staubach was only a junior. He'd be playing for the Midshipmen again next season. But he had gone to prep school for an extra year and since his original class was graduating, he was eligible for the draft as a future.

But what a long future! Besides staying at the Naval Academy for another year, Roger Staubach had a four-year commitment to the service. And anyone who knew Roger Staubach knew he didn't back down on his commitments. Thus, in early 1964, the Cowboys had drafted a quarterback who wouldn't be available to play for them until the fall of 1969. That's a long wait for any man, and it is a proven fact that few athletes can approach their old form after a layoff of four years.

Why, then, did the Cowboys do it?

"Our philosophy," explained general manager Schramm, "in the latter rounds of the draft is to take a gamble, a gamble on greatness. We just hoped that someday Roger would be able to play football for the Cowboys. Of course, there was a chance he wouldn't be commissioned, but we knew we'd likely have to wait five years. We felt strongly that Roger Staubach was a man worth waiting for."

Looking at Staubach's 1963 season at the Naval Academy, it becomes crystal clear why the Cowboys drafted him. As a junior, "Roger the Dodger" set the college football world on fire. He was the winner of both the Heisman Trophy and the Maxwell Award, the two top prizes given to the best college player in the land. He was everybody's All-America, and he led his team to a 9-1 record and a New Year's Day game with Texas in the Cotton Bowl. His coach, Wayne Hardin, called him simply "the greatest football player I've ever seen."

His individual record was equally phenomenal.

Roger completed 107 of 161 passes in that 1963 season, for a completion percentage of .664, and 1,474 yards. In addition, he rushed for 418 yards, and led his team to a season-ending rout of Army.

He was the complete quarterback, a pinpoint passer, a scrambler who knew no equal, and a devastating runner, as elusive as he was strong. He controlled a football game like no quarterback Navy had ever seen. In fact, his 1963 season is generally regarded as one of the greatest ever by a college football player anywhere. The way he played, a pro team would probably have waited ten years to get him.

The Middies had a tough schedule in 1963. Coach Hardin took his team up against the likes of Michigan, S.M.U., Pittsburgh, Notre Dame, Duke, and Army. None of that fazed the mighty Staubach. Roger the Dodger was the same elusive personage against them all. Maybe they should have called him the magician, or the invisible man. At least, that's how he must have seemed to the frustrated defensive players who had to chase him all year.

"One thing I learned about Roger," said coach Hardin, "was to let him have his head when he was on the field. When he started to break a pattern, I couldn't tear my hair. He had such great ability, and was such a winner, that I just had to believe that what he was doing would come out all right in the end."

It usually did. Jolly Roger, as he was also called, was never reluctant to go off on a trip of his own. He'd often run to one side of the field, then the other, sidestepping attempted tackles, zigzagging his way past frenzied defenders, spinning, dancing, jumping, twisting, faking. And the chase was usually in vain. It was a game in which the hunted outwitted the hunters. He might scramble for 30 seconds or more, then finally spot an open man, crank his arm, and rifle the ball to paydirt, while his impatient pursuers gasped for breath.

He had a style all his own, a style they said wasn't suited to pro ball, where the pocket passer still reigned supreme. But Roger Staubach was a determined, dedicated young man. And he was a leader, an innovator, a winner. Tex Schramm and the Cowboys saw all these things. They were willing to wait. Sooner or later, they felt, the Jolly Roger would land for good. And Dallas would be the better for it.

The Dodger made his debut in a Cincinnati hospital on February 5, 1942, the only son of Robert and Elizabeth Staubach, both fine, upstanding members of their community. From the first, they taught their son the same values by which they lived their own lives, and young Roger quickly became deeply religious, honest, devoted, and dedicated to whatever enterprise he undertook.

And it didn't take him long to undertake an interest in sports. He started playing football, basketball, and baseball in the CYO leagues in Cincinnati and soon was exhibiting outstanding ability in all three. He went to St. John Evangelist Elementary School and was a good student, but his parents admitted that he always had one eye on the playground. And when he got out there, he'd play ball from morning to night, whichever sport was in season. They were all fine with him.

When he was seven, he began playing baseball on knothole teams which were co-managed by his father.

"Roger could do anything even then," his father says proudly. "We put him wherever we needed a player on that particular day. I remember one time we had to have a catcher. Roger had never played there before, but he stepped in and did a fine job."

One thing that didn't make the grade with young Roger was music lessons. His mother wanted him to play the piano, so they hired a teacher to work with him.

"The boys drove the teacher crazy," Mrs. Staubach recalls. "They'd be out on the porch making all kinds of noise and waiting for Roger to finish. He couldn't wait to get outside either, so we finally called the whole thing off."

As a seventh grader at St. Paul, Roger began playing football. He could already carry the ball so they put him at halfback. He stayed at that position for two years, then entered Purcell High School, where he was moved to end his freshman year. The next season the coach made Roger his quarterback, and the change produced a strange reaction from the young Staubach.

"He came home and cried," says Mr. Staubach. "He really didn't like the idea. He enjoyed running with the ball even then and the Purcell coach didn't like his quarterbacks to run."

Roger really didn't have to worry, because the next season he was switched again, this time to defensive halfback. The coach liked his seniors to have the fun and glory of running the offense, while the juniors did the dirty work on defense. But by then Roger had taken a liking to being the quarterback and he was looking forward to returning to that position as a senior.

Return he did. Before long, it became obvious that Purcell High had a real superstar. Up to that time, Purcell signal-callers rarely ran with the ball. They would hand off, pitch out, or pass. Roger changed all that.

"Roger just ran around back there," one of his teammates said. "Five or six guys from the other team would be chasing him and no one could catch him. The fans went wild and Roger usually turned the play into a big gain."

Purcell High became a big winner, and in their traditional game with arch rival Elder High, Roger really set things on fire. With the defense looking for a pass, the lanky quarterback began scrambling. Then he was past the line of scrimmage and streaking for the sideline. Sidestepping and outmaneuvering several would-be tacklers, Roger streamed downfield on a 60-yard touchdown romp. It won the game and really put young Mr. Staubach on display as a quarterback with a future.

College offers began pouring in. Roger had a choice, of course. Wanting a good football school and still inclined to continue his Catholic education, he looked to Notre Dame as the only place for him. But the Irish were hesitant, and seemed reluctant to make any concrete offers. In fact, they discussed basketball with him, rather than football.

Other schools were more persistent. Woody Hayes, the coach at Ohio State, figured Roger would fit right in with his ground-oriented attack and made a determined, personal effort to land him.

"Mr. Hayes must have spent a fortune in phone calls," Mrs. Staubach said. "And everything he did was direct, not through an assistant. He spoke with Roger, visited him, and really showed a personal interest."

Purdue was also high on the list. Roger even went as far as to make a tentative acceptance there, but it was never anything concrete. Young Staubach did well academically and was also president of the student council at Purcell, so he was looking for more than a place to play football. That's where the Naval Academy came in.

Richard Kleinfeldt, a prominent Cincinnati resident, whose son had played football for Navy, was an ardent supporter of the Academy. He spoke to Roger about attending and then personally took him on a tour of the facilities.

"I think when Roger saw the Academy, he was convinced," Kleinfeldt said. "He realized that it was a place where he could play top-flight football, yet still get his education. And at the same time he could be serving his country. He felt very strongly about doing more in life than just playing ball."

So Roger made his commitment. But he had one more game as a high schooler. It was the annual North-South game featuring all the best seniors in the Cincinnati area.

"He ran wild," says Navy coach Wayne Hardin. "He was by far the best player on the field, on offense and defense, and these were kids from the whole of Cincinnati. I was overjoyed to see it. We were going to get quite a football player, someone I knew could turn our entire program around."

But it wasn't that easy. Two things happened. The first Roger shook off easily. After his great performance in the North-South game, Notre Dame approached him again, this time with an offer. Maybe there was a way he could realize his dream after all. But he said no. He'd already told the Academy that he would come there, and he refused to go back on his word.

The second he wasn't able to control. Roger didn't do well in English on his entrance exam. "I was never much of a reader and I guess my vocabulary was weak," he said. Anyway, Academy officials told him he'd have to go to prep school for a year and improve his English. Roger was depressed.

"I spent over a year talking to Roger at regular intervals." says Rick Forzano, current head coach at Navy, then the defensive backfield coach. "I had to convince him that prep school was the best bet. He was anxious to play ball and begin his education, but he realized the additional year of prep wouldn't hurt. And all the time, other schools were dangling scholarship offers in his face. A man of lesser character might have been tempted, but not Roger. Once he made up his mind, that was it."

At the New Mexico Military Institute, Roger was an immediate hero. He stepped in and led the junior college team to a 9-1 record, completing over 60 per cent of his passes and being named to the Junior College All-America first team. Major Bob Shaw, the head coach at NMMI, said that Staubach was a better player than John Unitas at the same level of development, and Shaw was a former assistant coach of the Baltimore Colts.

In addition to his gridiron prowess, Roger also was an all-conference and all-region basketball player, averaging 13 points a game. He made third team All-America as a centerfielder on the NMMI baseball team, batting .320 for the year. In between, he studied hard and the next fall entered the Naval Academy at Annapolis.

It didn't take long for the Jolly Roger to work his magic at the Academy. Taking charge of the plebe (freshman) team from the start, Staubach led the junior Middies to a fine 8-1 season, and served notice that Coach Hardin had some great talent on the horizon. Roger passed and ran defenses crazy, and it wasn't long before the Academy's Sports Information Director, Budd Thalman, tagged the young star, Roger the Dodger.

His sophomore year was one of great expectations, for both Roger and the team. But aside from football, he was finding life at Annapolis much to his liking.

Always devoutly religious, Roger continued to attend Mass daily, even though it meant getting up at 5:45 A.M. every day. Back at 6:30, making his bed and "squaring off" his room, he got set for a full day of activities that didn't end until midnight or thereabout, when he usually fell asleep over a book. He also had a girl, Marianne Hobler, a nurse in Cincinnati whom Roger had known since the first grade. The two planned to marry someday, but he knew that they couldn't be serious about it until he graduated from the Academy. So Roger and Marianne were "engaged to be engaged" for four years. But even that step took a great degree of soul searching on Roger's part. He views every phase of life with the utmost concern.

"I gave a lot of thought to preparing for the priesthood while I was in high school," Roger says. "I prayed very hard to find the right vocation. Finally I realized that I should get married someday and raise a family."

He accepted the almost monastic life at the Academy as being the right thing for him. It had to be that way. In fact, the big-time social whirl was one of the reasons he turned down Ohio State.

"It was just too worldly for me," Roger says. "There was too much happening all the time, too many social obligations. Don't get me wrong, I don't mean to criticize people for having fun there, but it wasn't what I wanted from college. I wanted to keep my sense of values in proportion."

Fortunately for the Academy, his sense of values included playing the best brand of football he could. As soon as he came out for the varsity, his sophomore year, Coach Hardin knew he had a winner.

"Quarterbacks have to be leaders," the coach said. "They have to show that quality both on and off the field. Roger Staubach is a high class gentleman with the right ideas and morals. He's a born leader."

There was just one problem, something Hardin had to work out in his own mind. "We had a senior quarterback the year Roger was a sophomore," Hardin recalls. "His name was Ron Klemick and he was a good ballplayer. In fact, the season before, he was instrumental in taking a mediocre team to a fine 7-3 record."

He had been outstanding. He threw well and also was a good leader.

"Now I knew Roger was ready. He could step in and just take over. But I wouldn't just kick Klemick in the behind and tell him to sit down. It wasn't right. I told Roger this and told him he'd have to earn the starting position. He said that was fine with him, so we started the season with Klemick at quarterback and Staubach on the bench."

Roger played only four minutes of Navy's 1962 opener against Penn State. It must have been frustrating, because the Nittany Lions buried the Middies, 41-7. The next week, Staubach didn't get in at all, as Klemick led his team past a mediocre William and Mary club, 20-16. Then Minnesota got hold of Navy and won easily, 21-0, with Roger seeing just two minutes of action. Klemick wasn't doing the job and the handwriting was on the wall.

Minutes before the opening kickoff in the Cornell game the following week, coach Hardin made an abrupt decision.

"Roger, warm up. You're starting today," he said.

The Jolly Roger put on his helmet, peeled off his jacket to reveal the number 12 on the back of his jersey, and started throwing the football. A new era in Navy football was about to begin.

With Staubach in the lineup, the Middies jumped to life. Roger quickly added a crispness to the attack that had been missing thus far. He handed the ball to his backs just as they burst past him into the holes. When he went to pass, he dropped back quickly, spotted his receiver, and drilled the ball home. When a play was broken ... well ... that's when he really went to work, showing the scramble-stuff that would drive opponents crazy.

Every time Roger took off on one of his journeys, the Cornell players pursued in vain. The elusive number 12 wiggled his shoulders and performed magic with his feet. Eight times he took off overland in that first game, and he picked up 89 yards. His passing was even more impeccable, as he completed nine of 11 for 99 yards and an .818 percentage. He easily led the Midshipmen past their outgunned opponents, 41-0.

"Roger was just super," Hardin said. "He was even better than we thought he'd be. There was no containing him, no way at all. I think Klemick understood. We had a superplayer who was going to improve with each passing week. He couldn't be kept on the bench any longer."

The Jolly Roger continued his rampage, leading the Middies past Boston College and Pittsburgh. In the latter game he was perfect, completing eight out of eight passes for a fantastic 192 yards and a touchdown. That's an average of 24 yards gained per pass. Amazing.

Then Navy hit a dry spell. Hardin just didn't have enough depth or experience, and Staubach couldn't do it alone against the power teams. First Notre Dame toppled the Middies, 20-12; then Syracuse did a real job, 34-6, and Southern Cal completed the trio of losses, getting by, 13-6. This was a close one. The Trojans were ranked among the top teams in the country, but Roger gave them fits. He was 11 for 17 passing, and scrambled for 113 yards and a touchdown. The game put the Middies back on the beam and got them ready to meet Army in the season's finale.

There's no way anyone can predict the outcome of an Army-Navy game. The rivalry goes way back to 1890 and when the two teams meet, it's no holds barred. So anxious are both service academies to win the annual clash that coaches are sometimes the first casualties of battle.

Coming into the 1962 game, Navy had beaten Army three straight times. Exit Army coach Dale Hall, despite a good overall record. Enter Paul Dietzel, a young, dynamic coach from Louisiana State with no prior service connections. But Dietzel had built a football power at LSU and had introduced three-platoon football to the land. He had a White Team, his regulars who played both ways for about half the game. Then there was the Go Team, offensive specialists; and the famed Chinese Bandits, his defensive platoon. This way, he used almost all his players and each unit had a pride and a drive all its own.

Army arrived at Philadelphia's Municipal Stadium on December 1, with a 6-3 record, a mark that included wins over Penn State and Syracuse, two teams that had beaten the Middies badly. Navy, on the other hand, was just 4-5, and needed the game for a break-even year. But records mean nothing when these two teams meet.

With President John Kennedy among the 98,616 spectators, Navy drew first blood when an Army punt attempt resulted in a bad pass from center and a safety. The Cadets then drove into Navy territory, only to miss a field goal try from the 27. That's when Staubach went to work.

He passed 39 yards to Ed Merino, then tossed a five-yarder to Bob Teall. He let his backs carry deeper into Army land, then scrambled for eight more himself. With the ball on the Army 12, Jolly Roger dropped back and calmly hit Neil Henderson with a 12-yard scoring pass. The touchdown, coupled with the earlier safety, gave the Middies an 8-0 lead.

The next time Navy got the ball, Staubach struck again. Chinese Bandits notwithstanding, he passed 16 yards to end Jim Campbell. Another quick toss to Dave Sjuggerud found the mark for ten more. Then the backs took over, running the ball to the Army 20. Staubach took the ensuing snap and rolled out to his right. When he saw his receivers covered, he began slithering past Army tacklers like a snake. He side-stepped one, spun off another, faked a third right onto his back, and when he crossed the goal line there were still no hands on him. It was a brilliant run and the extra point gave Navy a 15-0 lead.

Army came back to make it 15-6, but Roger the Dodger wasn't through yet. Early in the third quarter, he eluded two onrushing linemen and coolly tossed a 65-yard scoring strike to fullback Nick Markoff, who was all alone when he caught the ball on the Navy 45 and ran the rest of the way home. It was a great call by Roger, who isolated his back in the middle and hit him with a bullet. The kick made it 22-6, in favor of Navy.

In the final session, Roger led another long drive, firing a 48-yard strike to Campbell, and hitting on two short pitches to halfback Johnny Sai before taking it in himself from the two. Navy led, 28-6, and for all purposes, the game was over right there. The final was 34-14, and the Middies sent the cadets back to West Point in defeat.

As for Roger, he completed an amazing 11 of 13 passes for 188 yards and two touchdowns. He was also Navy's leading rusher with 24 yards on 14 carries, and scored two more touchdowns via the ground. It was a scintillating performance. Roger had finally made believers out of them all.

"Our line just couldn't put a good rush on him," Dietzel said. "When we crashed with our outside linebackers, he spotted them and took off around the end. And we sure as heck couldn't catch him.

"Four or five times I thought we were going to nail him for about a 20-yard loss. But he'd always seem to wind up with a 15-yard gain instead. He's really an incredible football player."

Steve Belichick, Navy's chief scout, confirmed the fact that Staubach had an uncanny knack for spotting onrushing linemen. "He has terrific peripheral vision," Belichick said. "He sees those guys coming from the sides and even spots the ones behind him. I don't know exactly how he does it all the time, but he moves just fast enough to get out of the way."

Staubach himself didn't have much to say after the game. But when a reporter asked him what happened to the Chinese Bandits, he answered with his usual quiet honesty. "I really can't say it made any difference. I didn't know when the Bandits were in the game and when they weren't."

It was a cinch that Staubach was in the game, though, and with the same basic team returning, the

Midshipmen anxiously awaited the start of the 1963 season.

But even before it started, the 6-2, 195-pound signal-caller was the talk of the land. He hadn't made any major All-American teams as a sophomore because his season didn't start until the fourth game, but everyone was predicting big things for him in '63. The Academy foresaw the fame that was going to come his way and took steps to protect him.

Soon after the opening game there was a general ban on Staubach interviews. Publicity director Budd Thalman explained it this way.

"We decided before the season that this kid was going to be in the spotlight. If we allowed writers and photographers in at all, Roger would have no time for himself. You understand that a midshipman has very little free time anyway. We didn't want to take that away from him, so we put the pressure on ourselves."

And by midseason, the prophecy was coming true. Hardin, himself a reticent and secretive man concerning his football team, said, "More people would like to see Roger right now than any other sports celebrity. If we opened the doors, I'll bet there would be nearly 5,000 writers and photographers waiting to get in."

Roger's statistics from 1962 served notice. He had completed 67 of 98 passes for 966 yards and a completion percentage of .684. Seven tosses went for touchdowns, and he scored seven more times on the ground, having annexed 265 yards on 85 carries.

He started the next season right where he left off, completing 17 of 22 passes in a 51-7 rout of West Virginia. The next week he was 12 of 17 for 206 yards, and he added another 91 running in a 28-0 blanking of William and Mary. Then Roger led the Middies into their first tough one of the year against Michigan.

It was a hard-fought game from start to finish, and when it ended, the passing of Roger Staubach had taken its toll. The Jolly Roger riddled the Wolverine defense for 14 completions in 16 tries for 237 yards and two scores. He also ran the ball 18 times, gaining 70 yards in a one-man show that had the football world talking once more. P.S.: Navy won, 26-13.

Everyone looked to Annapolis. That's where the action was. That's where Roger Staubach was calling the plays.

Even his coach couldn't believe what was happening. "I've just got to realize that this guy is something special," Hardin confessed. "In the Michigan game they're leading us by a touchdown with less than a minute remaining in the first half. The ball's close to midfield and he calls two straight running plays. I wondered what was going on. The next thing I know he's got the ball up in the air and we've got a touchdown." (Staubach had thrown a 43-yard touchdown pass.)

"Then in the second half we drive to their 18. I watch him roll to the left, then back to the right. Then he's all over the place. Suddenly he's rolling past me and I'm standing on the 50. I was ready to have a nervous breakdown. Then he gets hit and he's parallel to the ground. I figure it's all over. Suddenly he flicks his arm and tosses a pass to Donnelly, who runs it back upfield and we get a one-yard gain. I couldn't believe it."

But the party ended the following week. Navy traveled to the Cotton Bowl in Dallas to meet Southern Methodist University. It was one of the roughest college games ever played, and Roger the Dodger had to pull out every stop just to survive. And he still found time to be magnificent.

Early in the first quarter, a big SMU tackle cracked into Staubach from the blind side. It was one of the few times he didn't see an onrushing lineman. Roger went to the sidelines, holding his left shoulder. The official diagnosis was a stretched nerve, but the Dodger shook off the pain, and returned to bull his way through the center of the Mustang line for a score.

SMU scored two touchdowns on the ground, but Roger came right back to set up a score with a nifty scramble inside the ten. He threw for a two-point conversion and had the Middies back on top, 18-13.

When the second half started, SMU again began gang-tackling the Navy quarterback. It was as if they were going after the bad shoulder, trying to put him out of the game.

"It's the only time I ever saw him angry," Hardin said. "He felt they were taking cheap shots. They hurt his shoulder, bloodied his face, and scratched at him every time his helmet came off. But he never complained."

Ignoring the pain in his left shoulder, Staubach drove his team into SMU territory again, this time tossing a touchdown pass to one of his ends and giving the Middies a 25-13 lead. They seemed well in command.

But the Mustangs had a world of speed, and the Navy defense couldn't cope with it. Two long touchdown runs turned the game around, and before you could say, "Raise the Jolly Roger," SMU led, 26-25.

Staubach went back to work. He circled the right end, stutter-stepping past tacklers. Then he was hit by three, four, five Mustangs. He didn't get up. The trainer came out and waved smelling salts under his nose. Minutes later he was standing over his center again, driving the team to the two-yard line, where they were stopped and forced to settle for a field goal. It was 28-26, with just 2:52 left, and the battered Staubach slumped on the bench, hoping his defense would do the rest.

They didn't. SMU rolled for 70 yards in just four plays and were suddenly on top, 32-28, with two minutes left. Navy got the kickoff back to the 40, but still had to go another 60 yards to win it.

In one of the most courageous drives ever seen, the Navy moved upfield under the proddings and personal heroics of its great quarterback. On the first play Roger romped around right end for 16 yards. Then he passed for 14 more. Setting up quickly, he cranked the arm and released. Complete! Another 12 yards. He dropped back again. This time his receivers were covered, so he took off right up the middle and bedazzled the SMU defenders for 15 yards. Now there were just two seconds left on the clock.

The huge Cotton Bowl crowd was hushed. The snap. Staubach dropped back. He fired into the end zone. There was receiver Ed Orr reaching for the ball. He had it ... NO ... he dropped it! The pass skittered off his fingertips. Navy had lost its first game of the year.

Though he'd never admit it, Staubach came out of the game a winner. Every adjective in the book was used to describe his performance. The game solidified his reputation as the most exciting performer in college football. He had everything it takes. If there was ever a question of his courage or his ability to play with pain, that, too, was eliminated.

Navy wasn't to lose another one all year, topping Notre Dame 35-14, and beating Dietzel and Army once more, 21-15. Roger was the star straight through. He finished the regular season with 107 of 161 passes for 1,474 yards and a .664 completion percentage. He was everybody's All-America and took every major award there was.

When he received the Heisman Trophy in New York a week after the Army game, Roger was asked the inevitable question for the first time. Did he plan to play pro ball?

"I can't really say for sure at this time whether I'll play pro ball," he answered. "I've still got a year and a half at Annapolis, then four years of Naval service to think about it. So I'm really concerned with my future in the Navy right now."

Staubach was only the fourth junior in football history to win the coveted Heisman Trophy, and that was just one of the factors that gave unbeaten and top-rated Texas a little more impetus in the 1964 Coton Bowl game. That's right, the Middies got the bid by virtue of their fine 9-1 season. They were ranked right behind the Longhorns, and the game was billed as deciding the mythical National Championship.

Mighty Texas was just too much for the men of Annapolis. The game was won in the line, as the huge Texas tackles, ends, and linebackers stayed on Roger's back all day. He managed to pass for 228 yards, completing 21 of 31, but he couldn't take off on any of his patented scrambles. In fact, he was caught behind the line so often that he wound up with minus 47 yards rushing. The final score was 28-6. The Midshipmen were beaten decisively.

After the game, Staubach showed he still had a sense of humor. Someone had once said that "nobody knows what he's going to do except Staubach and God." Roger picked up this line and added to it.

"The way he rushed me in the Cotton Bowl game," Roger said, "I think you can say that God, Staubach, and Scott Appleton know what I'm going to do." Appleton was the mammoth Texas tackle who spent the day knocking Roger to the ground.

But nothing could take the luster off Roger's 1963 season. That was fortunate, because in 1964 his luck ran out. Before the season started, Wayne Hardin said his star would be better than ever. "He's more mature, older, and stronger," said Hardin, and few could argue with him off past performances. Navy lost some key men through graduation, but there was no reason to believe that the Middies wouldn't have a formidable team again.

Then it happened, in the first quarter of the very first game against Penn State. Roger was sandwiched between two Penn State defenders and slammed to the ground. When he got up, all the muscles in his right leg from the calf to the thigh were torn. There was also damage to the Achilles' tendon. He wouldn't be one hundred per cent all year. Roger the Dodger had lost his trump card.

"Roger wasn't the only one," Hardin said. "We had key personnel out at one time or another all year. I thought we had the potential to be great and we ended up losers.

"I really felt bad about Roger. He couldn't walk or run right all season, but he hung in there. Anyone else might have called it a year, but he wanted to help the team all he could. As a consequence, whenever he did start healing, he'd get racked up all over again."

Hardin's lament tells the tale. The team never got started. It won its first two, then went into a tailspin, losing five of its next six while tying the other. Dietzel and his Army team turned the trick, 11-8, in the finale, and the Middies finished the 1964 season with a lack-luster 3-6-1 mark.

A look at Roger's statistics is very revealing. He missed one game entirely, played just a few minutes in two others, yet he threw the ball more than the season before, completing 119 of 204 passes for 1,131 yards and just four touchdowns. His passing percentage dropped to .583, but his .636 career average is still the best in NCAA history.

The big change was in his rushing totals. Scrambling was always a big part of Staubach's game, but the leg injuries severely limited him, explaining the increased passing. He was officially credited with 104 carries for minus ... yes, minus ... one yard rushing. His only real big game was the second-to-last encounter of the season. He regained something of his old magic as the Midshipmen toppled Duke, 27-14. In that game, the Dodger compiled 21 of 30 passes for 217 yards and carred the ball 17 times for another 91 yards. He showed that when sound, he was still the best in the business. The following week he lost to the Army and his college career was over.

There were so many superlatives used to describe Roger Staubach by the end of the 1963 season that most were used up now. He was the first sophomore in Naval Academy history to win the coveted Thompson Trophy, "awarded to the Midshipman who has done the most during the current year for the promotion of athletics at the Naval Academy." Then as a junior, he won everything in sight, was named to every team in sight, and proclaimed the greatest collegiate football player in the land, maybe the best ever.

So after the injury-filled season of 1964, the questions became routine. What now, Rog? The pros, the Navy? Both, neither? Etc., Etc.

The facts were simple enough. Unless Roger got married, flunked his courses, or failed to pass his physical, he was committed to four years of service. He and Marianne were engaged, but wouldn't be married until after graduation. He wasn't about to flunk any courses, and his football injuries weren't so severe that he wouldn't pass the physical.

Roger spiced up the speculation by signing an optional contract with the Dallas Cowboys. It was a three-year pact, covering the years 1969-1972. He wouldn't be eligible until then. When it meant was that if he decided to play pro ball in 1969, the contract would automatically go into effect. If he decided to remain in the Navy, it was voided. He even got some regular payments from the Cowboys. If he played, the money would be part of his bonus. If not, the Cowboys just lost it. That's how much they wanted him.

"Roger will make it if he wants to," said Wayne Hardin as a parting shot. "He matured a great deal at Navy. He was more aware of the game and reacted to situations much better his last year. He learned to wait more and execute the play, rather than just taking off and improvising immediately. His arm was getting stronger and stronger. I think he could have made it big in the pros right away.

"Now he's got the layoff, but I don't think that will hurt him if he retains his desire. A man reaches mental, emotional, and physical maturity at the age of 29. So Rog has the time. He's just too good for his skills to erode completely."

And he left to fulfill his obligation. Goodbye, Roger! In his absence, the team that had drafted him went about the business of becoming a powerhouse. By 1966, the Cowboys were atop the Eastern Division of the NFL, and they have stayed there every year since. They had all-stars at every position and one of the league's better quarterbacks in Dandy Don Meredith. The name Staubach was all but forgotten.

Where was he? Well, first there was a year stateside, training as a supply officer.

"My first year away from the Academy, I missed football terribly," he said. "The whole thing: the competitiveness, the crowds, my teammates. It all seemed so far in the past."

Then it was off to Vietnam for a year, where there

were other things to think about. One day he got a small package from the States. It was "The Duke," the official football of the National Football League. The Cowboys had sent it to him as a present. Tex Schramm and Tom Landry hadn't forgotten.

"When I have the time and some guys to play catch with, I throw the ball about 400 times a day," Lieutenant Staubach said. "I intend to stay in the best shape I can and then make a fair decision about my future.

"I really don't see any physical problems. But the lost time will cost me valuable experience. If I play with the Cowboys, I'll be a 27-year-old rookie. But since I'm a quarterback, I'll have a lot of playing time left, maybe ten years or so. It's not like that with a halfback or lineman. If they lose a step, they lose a career. But a quarterback's biggest asset is his arm. That's why I'm throwing all the time. And I do some isometric exercises. Right now, I'd say my arm is the strongest it's ever been, and that includes my days at Annapolis."

In Vietnam, Roger was a freight terminal officer, in charge of unloading supplies. He had over 130 sailors, 61 Vietnamese, and two other officers under him. He wasn't involved in any direct action, but was once caught in a mortar barrage that killed one man and wounded three. One of the shells struck about 200 yards from the bunker that he was in.

From the war zone, he returned to Pensacola to finish his hitch. There he found himself playing football again, this time with the base team which had a schedule of nine small colleges and the Quantico

Marines. He slowly started getting his old wheels back in shape.

In the summer of 1966, he asked the Navy for a ten-day leave so he could participate in the Cowboy rookie camp at Thousand Oaks, California. It was granted, and after three years, Roger the Dodger was back in a big-time football uniform.

Roger joined the Cowboy rookies and tried not to attract too much attention. But when the Cowboys' yearlings went up against the San Francisco 49er first-year candidates, Staubach could stay in the background no longer.

Suddenly it was center stage all over again, not Annapolis, but it might as well have been. Roger rolled out, he scrambled, he ran, and he threw. Three times he connected with receivers in the 49er end zone. He completed 55 per cent of his passes and drove the young Frisco defenders crazy with his dazzle. Sideline observers who hadn't gotten the word asked in awe, "Who's that kid?"

When it was over, Roger returned to Pensacola and to the final eleven months of his hitch. But he had tasted pro football for the first time and was enthusiastic.

"Being out there with the Cowboy rookies really sold me on pro football," he told a reporter. "I kept myself in good shape the past three years. My arm's strong and the other things were coming back to me very quickly. I don't think I've reached my prime yet. So as far as I'm concerned, the good years are still ahead of me."

Roger was more talkative now than in his Academy days, when he had been virtually shielded from reporters. And he proved to be a most willing, though still soft-spoken subject. He told reporters that if he had come to the Cowboys' camp and found he had nothing left, he would have remained definitely in the Navy. Now, unless there was a national emergency, he was due to be released in June of 1969, just in time for the next regular training camp.

There were others enthusiastic over Roger's return to action. One was Tom Landry, the Dallas coach, and not a man given to wholesale praise.

"If last week was a true indication of his future, then we think he's an excellent prospect," Landry said. "What surprises me is that he doesn't seem to have lost anything by his long layoff. He throws the ball well, in fact, he's the kind of thrower you need in professional football. His arm was a lot stronger than we thought it would be. He was impressive on the sideline patterns, and that's always the mark of a good quarterback. Plus he still has the ability to run and scramble. I'm just sorry that we couldn't keep him here this year."

The Cowboys' public relations director, Curt Mosher, used even more superlatives in his praise of the Dodger.

"He's fantastic, just fantastic," Mosher said. "He was something else out there, wasn't he? He just went out and tore up the field. It's hard to believe he's been away for three years. Believe me, he's got some kind of future here. I think he can really make it big."

When Roger was set to report to the Cowboys, there were three veteran quarterbacks ahead of him. Don Meredith was number one, and at age 31, he seemed to have another seven or eight years ahead of him. Then there was Craig Morton and Jerry Rhome, two youngsters from the same graduating class as Roger. Yet they had picked up valuable experience by playing in spots and learning on the sideline. Staubach would be number four.

Then things began happening. First Rhome was traded—the Cowboy brass felt Morton had the better future. Then there was a real shocker. Without warning, Don Meredith notified the Cowboys that he was retiring. He'd had it. Dallas had lost the NFL championship to Green Bay in the final seconds two years running. Then they were beaten in the divisional playoffs by Cleveland. Meredith had had enough. The fans booed him and the opposition pounded him. He opted for a broadcasting career. In a dramatic turn of events, Craig Morton was the number one Dallas quarterback and his alternate was the rookie Staubach. The untried rookie Staubach.

"I'm confident in myself," Roger said. "I know I won't be number one immediately, but I want to make the team and find out what I can do.

"I gave up a career when I left the Navy. That should prove my confidence. But I'll never look back and regret it. If I hadn't tried to play pro ball now I'd spend the rest of my life wondering if I could have."

It wasn't long before everyone in the Cowboy camp was aware of Staubach's dedication. He worked hard and studied hard, determined to make up for lost time and regain the skills quickly that had made him such a great star at Navy. When Roger said he could run the 40-yard dash faster than the 4.9 seconds he did at Navy, few doubted him. Said one member of the Cowboys' staff:

"If you want Roger to do 4.75, just put him in there with a guy who does 4.8. Then he'll do 4.75."

As for Roger, his sound football mind made it easy for him to pick up the complex Cowboy offense. The thing he worried about was reading defenses.

"That will be a problem, recognizing defenses so you can change the play at the line of scrimmage. It's something you just can't do without experience. I just hope I get the chance to pick up the experience."

The first chance he got would be an experience, all right, one he'd never forget. It took place in July of 1969, and was the Cowboys' first rookie game against the yearlings of the Oakland Raiders. The Raider defensive candidates must have taken a cue from their veterans. One Oakland writer tapped them "The Eleven Angry Kids," a parody of the nickname given the Raider varsity defensive unit. Anyway, the angry kids really did a job on Roger Staubach.

When he dropped back to pass, they were around him like flies, and he had to run for his life. That resulted in hurried and off-balance passes, or throws that missed the receiver completely. By contrast, the Oakland rookie signal-callers, Ken Stabler and Eldridge Dickey, looked like seasoned veterans and the young Raiders romped 33-0.

"My timing was way off," Roger said afterward. "I overthrew guys and did a lousy job, that's all. I wasn't confused. Their secondary was quick and their line tough. I just didn't do a good job."

Coach Landry defended his rookie. "Roger's going to be great," the coach said, "but right now his mind's cluttered with our offense. He's trying to learn everything at once. He knows now that he's going to be our number two quarterback, not three or four, so he's pressing a bit."

Although Roger completed just two of 14 passes for 21 yards, he ended up as the team's leading ground gainer with 74 yards on only five carries. That was encouraging. He hadn't lost his ability to scramble and run, so his legs were still with him. The arm was already strong, so the timing and poise would come.

Roger kept working, through training camp and into the exhibition season. But Craig Morton was inheriting the number one spot for the first time and needed the work, too. So it was Craig who saw the bulk of the playing time in the exhibitions. Meanwhile, Staubach kept learning.

"I know I can still scramble," he said, "but I'm learning to be a drop-back passer. That's what it takes to be a professional quarterback. I'd still like to release the ball a little faster, and I've got to get used to reading defenses."

Ray Renfro, who coached the Cowboy receivers, said that Staubach surprised the coaches with his accuracy on short passes and his power on long bombs.

"He throws it 40 or 50 yards on a line," Renfro said. When asked how long it would take for Staubach to be a starter, he replied, "It will probably be a year or two before he has the experience to be a top quarterback, but there's no doubt that he has all the physical tools to do it."

But the football has strange ways of bouncing sometimes. Shortly before the Cowboys' 1969 opener with the St. Louis Cardinals, Morton injured a finger.

The word was he wouldn't be ready in time. The Cowboys' starting quarterback would be Roger Staubach.

"Coach Landry was really nervous before that first game," Roger recalls. "I don't think he liked rookie quarterbacks and he was really worried about how the team would do. I thought I'd break the ice, so I went up to him with a big smile on my face and said, 'Gee, coach ... just think ... only a year ago I was playing quarterback for the Pensacola Garhawks against Middle Tennessee. Now I'm starting against St. Louis.' Well, he just gave me a long look, turned, and walked away."

Landry needn't have worried. The game was in capable hands. With the coach sending the plays in from the bench, Staubach ran the club cautiously, but well. Sticking to basic football and relying on precision execution, Dallas methodically destroyed the Cardinals. Roger made few mistakes. He handed off smoothly and passed well. The Cowboy defense did the rest, stopping the Cards in their tracks, and when it ended Dallas was on top, 24-3.

It made a great Cinderella story for the press. Rookie Staubach, away from football for four years, starts the first NFL game he plays in and leads his team to a victory. In fact, he made it look easy, and some said he was going to take up right where he left off after the great season of 1963. Even Roger breathed a sigh of relief when it was over. His confidence was rewarded and he looked forward to seeing more action.

Unfortunately, Landry didn't feel the same way. He acknowledged that Roger had done a fantastic job in his first game, but quickly reaffirmed his intention to use Craig Morton as his quarterback. He stuck to his word. Roger didn't start another game all year, and Morton, despite a sore elbow that severely hampered his ability to throw, stayed at the helm right through another divisional playoff loss to the Browns.

When 1970 rolled around, Staubach was hoping for more playing time. He got it, but not much more. He started three games that year, only when Morton was below par, and the Cowboys won two of them. Roger threw 82 passes and completed 44 for 542 yards and two touchdowns. But he was sacked by defensive players 19 times and threw eight interceptions.

Despite this, he managed to gain 221 yards on 27 carries, an 8.2 average, and was the Cowboys' number four runner. That might have been the problem. Roger wasn't staying in the pocket and Landry didn't like it. He was scrambling, hurrying his tosses, and playing a helter-skelter game that didn't go in the pros. He was making costly mistakes in between brilliant flashes. One of these days he was bound to put it together.

The 1970 season was another frustrating one for the team. They won their division with a 10-4 mark, then topped Detroit 5-0, and San Francisco 17-10, to get into the Super Bowl. It was the goal they'd always sought.

But they'd done it on defense. Morton was soundly booed by the fans and criticized in the press. His arm still wasn't right. When the Colts whipped the Cowboys in the super game, 16-13, it marked the fifth straight year the powerful Dallas team was in the playoffs but didn't make it to the title. The fans and press clamored for a change.

So did Staubach. He had served his apprenticeship. He was 29 years old and felt he was ready.

"I'm extremely hungry for a starting football job," he told reporters. "I think I can be a starter for seven or eight years, preferably at Dallas, but if not, then somewhere else. If things don't work out this year, I want to be traded. Coach Landry knows about my feelings. I've spoken with him about it."

Landry was his usual evasive self. "I'm not worried about my quarterback situation," he said. "Either one of them (Morton or Staubach) can do the job. So I don't feel I have to make a decision because right now I plan on alternating them. Neither is clearly ahead of the other."

But then in the next breath, he said, "If Roger can't beat out Morton this year, I'll probably trade him."

Well, alternating with someone isn't the same as beating him out of a job, and Staubach continued to say things that would make his position perfectly clear.

"It seems to me the players would rather have one quarterback, no matter who he is. They have to have a leader, someone they respect and have confidence in, someone they know will do the job. This won't happen if the coach is constantly alternating his quarterbacks. Then it becomes a guessing game and no one has confidence, including the two quarterbacks.

"As far as I'm concerned, I would love to determine the fate of the Cowboys this year. I feel I'm the man to take them to the Super Bowl!"

People kept coming back to Landry. Yes, he said,

Staubach was capable of starting. "Last year, he didn't have the experience. That's why I didn't use him in the playoffs or Super Bowl. I didn't think he was ready. This year he is."

Still the coach wouldn't commit. The exhibition season started and Morton looked like the same quarterback he had been for the past two years. His arm just didn't seem right. Meanwhile, Staubach was moving the team. Staying in the pocket longer and picking out his receivers with care, Roger the Dodger looked good. He started and played against the Colts, picking apart the famous Baltimore zone defense by hitting 12 of 17 passes for 193 yards and two touchdowns as the Cowboys won, 27-14.

After five exhibitions, the two quarterbacks had played about the same amount of time. And the comparison was an interesting one. Staubach had thrown six touchdown passes, Morton just one. And Jolly Roger had just one pass picked off, while Craig had thrown four interceptions. Who would you start?

Some said the rap was still Roger's scrambling. Landry just couldn't handle it. He was from the old school and a believer in smooth, sound execution. To him, a scramble was a broken play. He didn't want to hear stories like the one player-coach Dan Reeves told about Roger.

"I ran what we call a 'shoot' pattern," the veteran halfback said, "straight down the right sideline. Then I look back for the ball, but there's Roger scrambling to his left. So I cut clear across the field and look to him again. By this time he's on his way back to the right, so I turn around and sprint back again. Man, it seemed as if I was just running back and forth out there. He finally spots me and delivers and we gain 17 yards.

"That kind of stuff isn't easy on anybody. I remember a game in 1967 when we were playing the Vikings in the Cotton Bowl. Tarkenton was the quarterback then and the temperature that day was about 102 degrees. Well, he takes off on one of his scrambles and kept running back there for so long that we had to call time out when the play was over and give our defensive unit oxygen."

Landry probably left the room when he heard that one. But there was something else he had to keep in mind. Staubach was a winner. He'd always been, and of the four regular season games he'd started in two years, the Cowboys had won three.

Still, when the team opened against Buffalo, Morton was at the helm. It didn't last long. In came Staubach. But then Morton returned. Then Staubach. It was obvious now that Landry was planning to alternate his two quarterbacks, the thing Roger not only dreaded, but felt was bad for the team.

The coach began switching them indiscriminately. Then patterns started to emerge. He would switch them at the end of each quarter; after a while he changed it to each series of downs. Morale on the team was low once again.

Finally, on October 31, against the Chicago Bears, Landry reached the epitome of his little game. He alternated Morton and Staubach on every play, having his quarterback bring the next call in from the bench. It was ludicrous. Dallas lost to a mediocre Chicago team, 23-19. With the season already at the halfway mark, the Cowboys had a record of just 4-3 and trailed the upstart Washington Redskins by two games. Landry finally realized that something had to be done.

It just didn't make sense. Dallas had one of the most powerful teams ever assembled. Its running backs, Duane Thomas, Calvin Hill, and Walt Garrison all combined speed and power; the ends, Bob Hayes and Lance Alworth, were an equally dynamic duo. The offensive line boasted several all-pro performers, and the Doomsday Defense was right up there with the league's best. Yet the team wasn't winning.

Landry finally made his decision, and to this day can't or won't say why he made it. But he called Roger Staubach and informed him that from then on, he'd be the one and only starting quarterback for the Cowboys.

The news came as a shock, but it was music to Jolly Roger's ears. This was what he'd been working and waiting for the past two and a half seasons. A chance. A real chance. And he wasn't about to blow it. Landry would still call the plays, sending them in with his tight ends, Billy Truax and Mike Ditka, whom he now alternated on every play. But Staubach would remain the man taking the snap.

Roger debuted on November 7th, against the Cardinals at St. Louis. It was nip and tuck all the way, but Dallas prevailed, 16-13. The new quarterback ran a cool, competent show. He wasn't sensational, but the team won and perhaps the Cowboy fortunes were turning around.

The next week Dallas returned home and their oft-disappointed fans watched them with skepticism. They didn't have to worry. The Cowboys won easily over Philadelphia, 20-7. The following week it was the defense's show. They blanked the Skins, and Staubach played another errorless game in putting 13 points on the board. The final was 13-0, and the Cowboys were again tied for the number one spot.

Staubach was improving. He was staying in the pocket, running only when he had to, but running so well that the defenses were always aware of the threat. He beat the Rams, 28-21; buried the Jets, 52-10; and rolled over the Giants 42-14, before ending the regular season with a 31-12 victory over the Cardinals.

Seven straight wins, and the Cowboys had finished with an 11-3 mark and the NFC Eastern Division championship. Landry's move had paid dividends. Roger Staubach started seven times and was a winner seven times. And he didn't do it by luck.

He was a dominant figure and inspiring leader. Sure, the team had its share of superstars and many of them had had fine years, but few achieved the perfection that Roger had in so short a time.

When the final statistics were released, Jolly Roger was the leading passer in the entire National Football League. He had thrown the football 211 times, completing 126 for a .597 average. His passes gained 1,882 yards and were good for 15 touchdowns. In addition, he led the league with an .892 average gain per pass and had only four of his tosses intercepted. And even better than that, only one of his last 192 throws had been picked off. He was truly sensational.

It wasn't even that he stopped scrambling so much. He just learned to pick his spots. In fact, he picked them 41 times, gaining 343 yards, for an incredible 8.4 yards per carry. But even while Staubach's feats were being praised up and down the league, Dallas fans wouldn't be believers until the team proved itself in the playoffs. They'd failed too many times in the past for anyone to get excited now. Sure, Staubach was a revelation, all right, but winning the Super Bowl was the name of the game in Dallas, and that's all anyone wanted to know.

The first step in the ultimate quest wouldn't be easy. The Cowboys had to meet the mighty Vikings of Minnesota, a powerhouse team weak at maybe one position: quarterback.

That turned out to be the difference. Coach Bud Grant switched back and forth between Bob Lee, Gary Cuozzo, and Norm Snead, strangely reminiscent of the old days at Dallas. The three-man parlay didn't work, and the Dallas defense contained the Vikes all afternoon.

Staubach, in the meantime, was running his own show. He patiently engineered two long touchdown drives, and two more that resulted in field goals as Dallas won it, 20-12. Now it was on to phase two, the National Conference championship game with the San Francisco 49ers, a team that had gained the finals by tripping the Washington Redskins.

The 49ers were solid, but they would go only as far as their quarterback, John Brodie, would take them. In 1970, Brodie had a tremendous year and his club was expected to get into the Super Bowl. But San Francisco ran into the Dallas defense one Sunday, and its season ended right there. In 1971, Brodie wasn't as sharp. He was prone to interceptions and never really got in the good groove. Yet his team won its division and was once again on the brink of the big one.

The two teams played it cautiously. Brodie was having his problems finding receivers, and Staubach was following Landry's instructions from the bench. He engineered one touchdown drive and the Cowboys led, 7-3, at the half.

In the third period Dallas had the ball on its own 23, a third and seven situation. If Staubach didn't make it here, the 49ers could easily take control of the game. Billy Truax shuttled the play in from the bench and Roger brought his club to the line. He took the snap and dropped straight back to pass. He did it so nicely that he looked more like John Unitas or Y.A. Tittle than Fran Tarkenton. Scramblers just don't drop back that way.

He looked downfield. Then he saw a couple of 49er linemen drawing a bead on him. Instinctively, he took off. It might have been Army-Navy all over again, with Roger the Dodger under a full head of steam. He zigged to one side, then spun back to the other, avoiding two tacklers. He was still surrounded, so he began retreating ... to the ten, to the five, to his own three-yard line.

It was the kind of thing that Wayne Hardin had learned to live with, but it still gave Tom Landry fits. Just when it looked as though Staubach was trapped, he escaped once more and started moving upfield, wagging his shoulders from side to side, a running style that makes it look as if he's faking when there's no one to fake. Suddenly he was back over the 15, then the 20. Just when it seemed he would keep running, Jolly Roger pulled up short of the line of scrimmage and heaved a pass to Truax for a gain of 17 yards.

The exhausted 49ers regrouped. But Staubach had taken the starch out of their sails. He quickly snapped his team together and completed an 80-yard drive for the Cowboys' second touchdown. The 14-3 triumph was a tribute to the Dallas defense and to the field generalship of Roger Staubach.

And now there was one. In two weeks, the Cowboys would be going to New Orleans—to the Super Bowl. All that stood between Dallas and the ultimate victory was the Miami Dolphins.

Miami, an expansion team of just six years standing, already was on the brink of football supremacy. They had a fine young quarterback, Bob Griese, who led the AFC in passing and ranked second only to Staubach in the entire NFL. Their running duo of Larry Csonka and Jim Kiick rivaled closely the Cowboys' ground game; and Paul Warfield was as good a receiver as anyone in the game. Defensively, the Dolphins could be had, but the youngsters and veteran middle linebacker Nick Buoniconti had shut out the tough Colts just two weeks earlier. It looked like a hard game all the way.

The Dolphin offense knew it would have a difficult time, but figured it would put points on the scoreboard. Many thought the game would be decided by the Miami defense. Could it stop the Dallas attack, or more precisely, could it contain Roger Staubach?

Although Roger had proven himself a fine passer over the second half of the season, it was his running that worried the Dolphin defenders.

"Even if he doesn't scramble, you can't forget about

it," said defensive back Dick Anderson. "You're always aware that he might take off and you've got to be ready.

"The thing about Staubach is that he can take the mental advantage away from the defense. Say if you've got him second or third down and long yardage. You cover all the receivers perfectly and suddenly he runs the ball down your throat for a first down. He can make the big play any time. And if he doesn't do it passing, he'll run it at you."

End Bill Stanfill explained how Roger caused him to alter his normal defensive preparations. "We try to keep the quarterback enclosed in a triangle. With most quarterbacks, I can achieve this and still take an inside rush. But against a scrambler, an inside rush can be dangerous."

Finally it was Nick Buoniconti's turn. The veteran linebacker was the heart and guts of the Miami defense. He was the stabilizing factor; yet he, too, feared Jolly Roger.

"He wants to stay in the pocket and pass," quick Nick said. "But there's just no telling when he's liable to take off. If he runs, breaks his pattern, you've defeated him. But he can kill you even after you've defeated him.

"I remember seeing some films earlier in the week. We saw one play where the defense forced Roger to break the play and take off. Coach Shula told us that this is what we should try to do, make him run, take away the pass. Well, while the coach is telling us all about this, the film is still running and Staubach's scramble turns into a 40-yard touchdown run, with about six tacklers left sprawling behind, grabbing just air."

Even Shula was worried. "The 49ers did an excellent job of defensing the Cowboys," the coach said. "The one thing they couldn't do was contain Staubach."

But Roger kept telling everyone he didn't want to run. "The coach doesn't like me to run the ball," he said. "But I will if the opportunity is there. The way I see it, anytime a quarterback can run out of the pocket and throw, it can kill a defense.

"I know some defensive people around the league don't like me to run, and they tell me about it. Cedric Hardman of the 49ers is always threatening me. Things like he's gonna knock my head off if I run his way again. They say stuff my insurance man wouldn't want to hear."

Roger went on to say that he felt the Dallas offense was due for a big game and he wasn't worried about their lack of a big production day in the two playoffs. Asked if he minded Landry calling all the plays from the bench, the QB said no, but he wouldn't consider himself a complete quarterback until he did everything, including play selection and calling. No doubt about it, Staubach was a determined young man. He showed that when asked about the outcome of the game.

"When I have a goal in mind," he said, "nothing stands in my way."

Super Bowl VI took place on January 16, at Tulane Stadium in New Orleans, on a beautiful, sunshine-filled day.

Both teams started slowly. Then, midway through

the first period, Miami fullback Csonka fumbled and linebacker Chuck Howley recovered at the Dallas 46. It was Csonka's first fumble all year, and 12 plays later it led to a Mike Clark field goal. Dallas led, 3-0. Then in the second period, Dallas got the ball on the Miami 24 and started driving.

Staubach directed the team flawlessly. He handed off to Thomas and Garrison, and watched them cut back against the grain, trapping the speedy Buoniconti, and moving for good gains. Or he dropped back and dumped short swing passes to his backs and ends. He marched his team up the field, bit by bit, slowly taking the heart out of the Miami defense. With the ball on the seven, Roger dropped back, stayed in the pocket, and whipped a perfect pass to Alworth in the near corner of the end zone. Clark converted, and it was 10-0 game.

The Dolphins made one serious bid in the first half, and it ended with a Garo Yepremian 31-yard field goal to make the halftime score 10-3.

But the Cowboys were doing the job. The front four, George Andrie, Jethro Pugh, Bob Lilly, and Larry Cole, were stopping the vaunted Miami running attack cold. And the linebackers and tough defensive backfield had taken Warfield's favorite lanes away from him. When Griese tried a page from Staubach's scrambling book, he was hauled down by Lilly for a 29-yard loss. The Dolphins were clearly on the run.

In the third quarter, Dallas took it to the Dolphins again. Staubach led another drive, keeping the ball mostly on the ground. With the ball at the 45, Duane

Thomas cut back off the right side for 23 yards and a first down at the Miami 22.

Then the Cowboys got fancy. Flanker Bob Hayes came steaming around on a reverse and carried it to the six. Two plays later Thomas went bulldozing into the end zone. Clark's kick made it 17-3, and the Cowboys were slowly edging closer and closer to that elusive championship.

Miami knew it had to move fast. Griese started his club driving. He had a third and four on his own 49 and dropped back to pass. The young Dolphin signal-caller threw in the direction of his halfback, Jim Kiick. But he'd done that twice before on third down and Chuck Howley was waiting. The veteran line-backer picked the ball off and returned it 41 yards to the Miami nine. Now Dallas could really put it away.

This time it took Roger three plays. A play-action fake and perfect pass to tight end Mike Ditka from seven yards out did the trick. It was Jolly Roger's second touchdown pass of the afternoon and upped the score to 24-3. Dallas would have had more. Larry Cole jumped on a Griese fumble on the Dallas 16, and Staubach quickly moved his club all the way up-field to the Miami 20. On fourth down, Landry called for a field goal, but it was a fake, and holder Dan Reeves ran to the 13 and a first down.

Landry had waited six years for this. He was having some fun. He called an end-around for Ditka and the veteran receiver rambled to the one. That's where Dallas finally turned it over. Calvin Hill fumbled and Miami recovered to end the drive. But it didn't matter any more, the damage was done.

In the end, Landry was carried off the field. It was

a big moment for him and he flashed one of his infrequent smiles. The 24-3 score showed just who was the best team in pro football. The Cowboys left little doubt. They'd beaten three powerful clubs on the way to the greatest triumph in their history.

Who would have thought it ten games earlier, when Dallas was just 4-3, and seemingly faltering? Then a young man named Staubach was given the quarterback job. The Cowboys hadn't lost since.

That's right. Ten straight wins ... no losses. In fact, in his three years with the Cowboys, Staubach had a 16-1 record as a starter. You can't do much better than that.

His Super Bowl effort was typical. The one-time Navy lieutenant completed 12 of the 19 passes he attempted, for 119 yards and two scores. As usual, there were no interceptions. His club had gained a record 252 yards on the ground, so it's obvious how well Dallas mixed its plays and executed them. Staubach hadn't done it alone.

Yet big Ditka, who's seen the best of them play during his decade in the league, had this to say: "Roger's a great leader. He just doesn't quit. He does it by getting out there and doing it, without wasting words. He brought this team to life."

So it finally appeared that the Cowboys were Roger's team, that he was the leader, number one. He spent the off-season receiving the plaudits that go with being a Super Bowl hero. In 1972 Roger was ready to go again.

But in the third exhibition game he tried to run over Rams middle linebacker Marlin McKeever. *Bang!* There was one of those collisions that only pro footballers know. McKeever was knocked woozy, momentarily. But Roger had a separated right shoulder.

"The same thing that made him try to run over McKeever will be what brings him back," said Coach Landry.

But while Roger was recovering, Morton again became the number one QB and led the Cowboys into the playoffs. Roger was finally activated for the final few games, throwing only 20 passes and completing nine in the regular season. Then came the first playoff game against the San Francisco 49ers. The Cowboys trailed 28-16 with only 2:02 remaining, and Landry, on a hunch, switched from Morton to Staubach.

In a matter of seconds it was the old Jolly Roger, never better. He marched his club downfield and fired a 20-yard TD to Billy Parks. Then the club got the ball on an onsides kick, and Rog was back. He scrambled for good yardage a couple of times, then hit Ron Sellers with a 10-yard scoring pass. He had done it, pulled the game out of the fire in the greatest pressure comeback in Dallas history. The Cowboys won, 30-28, and went to the NFC title game.

That's where the rustiness showed through. Roger got the start and had a bad day. The Redskins won, 26-3, eliminating Dallas from Super Bowl competition.

"I'm going to devote next season to making up for this one," a disheartened Staubach said after the game.

He did. He won the number one job from Morton in pre-season and went on to have another great year, in fact, his first real full, start-to-finish, season. He got the Cowboys into the playoffs and finished as the top passer in the NFC.

He completed 179 of 286 for 2,428 yards and a 62.6 percentage. It was the old Staubach accuracy. He tied with Roman Gabriel for the most TD passes in the NFL, 23, and had just 15 of his tosses intercepted. Many members of the great Cowboys dynasty were aging, and it didn't really come as a surprise when the team lost to Minnesota, 27-10, in the NFL title game. But no one could fault Roger; he had come all the way back. People have a tough time saying anything bad about Roger Staubach.

He's a devoted human being, devoted to God, his family, and his country. He believes in all the fine principles under which this country was founded. He's an honorable man who won't compromise his own ethics for anything. Yet he has survived and surfaced as a superstar in one of the toughest businesses in the world.

Yes, sir, Tex Schramm made a wise draft choice back in 1964. He said then that the Cowboys were willing to wait, willing to gamble on greatness. They waited all right—and they got themselves a leader and a winner. He was worth waiting for.

The Jolly Roger is once again flying high.

PRO STATISTICS

Jim Plunkett

Year	Att.	Comp.	Pct.	Yds.	TD	Int.	Ave. Gain
1971	328	158	.482	2,158	19	16	6.58
1972	355	169	.476	2,196	8	25	6.18
1973	376	193	.513	2,550	13	17	6.78
Totals	1,059	520	.491	6,904	40	58	6.52

Roman Gabriel

Year	Att.	Comp.	Pct.	Yds.	TD	Int.	Ave. Gain
1962	101	57	.564	670	3	2	6.63
1963	281	130	.463	1,947	8	11	6.93
1964	143	65	.455	1,236	9	5	8.66
1965	173	83	.479	1,321	11	5	7.64
1966	397	217	.538	2,540	10	16	5.82
1967	371	196	.528	2,779	25	13	7.50
1968	366	184	.503	2,364	19	16	6.49
1969	399	217	.544	2,549	24	7	6.39
1970	407	211	.520	2,552	16	12	6.27
1971	352	180	.511	2,238	17	10	6.36
1972	323	165	.511	2,027	12	15	6.27
1973	460	270	.587	3,219	23	12	7.00
Totals	3,773	1,975	.523	25,442	177	124	6.74

Greg Landry

Year	Att.	Comp.	Pct.	Yds.	TD	Int.	Ave. Gain
1968	48	23	.479	338	2	7	7.04
1969	160	80	.500	853	4	10	5.33
1970	136	83	.610	1,072	9	5	7.88
1971	261	136	.521	2,237	16	13	8.57
1972	268	134	.500	2,066	18	17	7.71
1973	128	70	.547	908	3	10	7.09
Totals	1,001	526	.525	7,474	52	62	7.47

Roger Staubach

Year	Att.	Comp.	Pct.	Yds.	TD	Int.	Ave. Gain
1969	47	23	.489	421	1	2	8.99
1970	82	44	.537	542	2	8	6.61
1971	211	126	.597	1,882	15	4	8.92
1972	20	9	.450	98	0	2	4.90
1973	286	179	.626	2,428	23	15	8.49
Totals	646	381	.590	5,371	41	31	8.31